The Gluten-F

Authentic Recipes from the New Dawn Kitchen

Dawn Grey, PhD, CHHP

The Gluten-Free Vegan Italian
Authentic Recipes from the New Dawn Kitchen
Dawn Grey, PhD, CHHP

Visit our website at www.newdawnkitchen.com

Library of Congress Cataloging-in-Publication Data

ISBN-10: 1453835326
EAN-13: 9781453835326

Printed in the United States of America

Acknowledgements

This is my third cookbook, and would not be possible without the encouragement of my readers of ***"New Dawn Kitchen: Gluten-Free, Vegan, and Easily Sugar-Free Desserts"***, and ***"The Virtuous Vegan"***, my clients, Facebook fans, and those of you who took the time to personally email me and thank me for sharing my recipes. There are a few others who deserve special mention, as without them, this book would not have been written:

The Daiya Cheese Company, for making the yummiest gluten-free, vegan cheeses on the planet. Before your products, my Italian food tasted like plastic. The pizza on the cover? That's Daiya!

To the makers of Mimic Crème, a heartfelt thank you for enabling me to make Alfredo, creamy soups, and the best coffee drinks I have had since I had to forfeit dairy.

My husband, Mark, who once again endured the kitchen messes and my talking out loud phases. This time, no exploding cakes! I love you.

Finally, to my feline friend, Twilight, aka Yogi Purrananda. We did it again. I know there are other books and cookbooks yet to come of our collaborative efforts. The Yogini Panini you say? You got it! Om. Purr. Om.

Table of Contents

To The Reader

The recipes contained within these pages are the result of many years of modifying and taste testing, by myself and those who would never consciously eat gluten-free or vegan. Most of the time, they had no idea they were eating, other than it was really good food.

It is not my goal to try to educate the public as to why they should eat gluten-free, vegan, or watch their sugar and sodium intake. While there is much I could say on these subject matters, this is a celebration of food and not a health guide. There is much that can be said about our need to eliminate chemicals and fast food from our diet, but that is not for me to say here. Instead, I chose to focus my attention on what you *can* have. To those that are gluten-free and/or vegan, I am here to provide you with options and not with excerpts of research and case studies. You bought this book because you or the recipient needs to eat this way.

It is my belief that while food is fuel, it is meant to be enjoyed and celebrated. Growing up in an Italian family introduced to me this mentality. There is no reason to ever eat something you do not like, nor do I believe you should ever eat food that taste less than delicious. However, for those like me, who are suddenly presented with an immediate reason to give up an entire food group, this can create quite a challenge.

These pages contain Italian recipes that I simply adore, and I believe you will, too. Feel free to modify according to your tastes. Use the shape of pasta or ingredients you can easily obtain.
Mangia!

Dawn Grey

Introduction

We have all experienced moments in our lives when we realize our lives have changed forever. These moments forever define our character. I believe it is not what happens to us but how we react to what happens to us that ultimately shapes our life experience. While I have had my ups and downs in life like anyone else, from dealing with a family member's chronic illness to my own struggles with weight, nothing has impacted my life more than the realization that there are some foods that I cannot eat without severe impact to my health and well-being: dairy, egg yolks, shellfish, and wheat and gluten containing foods (primarily limited to the cooler months of the year). While the omission of shellfish was no big deal, as I have been a vegetarian more on than off since age 17, the impact of losing wheat, gluten, and dairy were immense. I love vegetables and primarily eat vegan anyways, but wheat? What was I to do about bread? Pasta? What about baking?

I am the go to girl in my group when it comes to baking. I am not a baker by training or profession. However I have the knack in duplicating a dessert recipe if I take the time to eat it slowly, examine its texture, and carefully pay attention to its scent, color, and weight. I will even admit that I can create a recipe that often I myself cannot bake with initial success (hence the thank you to my husband and comment about exploding cakes) until I play with it a few times. But ultimately, I am the one who makes yummy treats, supports bake sales for schools and churches, and the one that everyone hopes will get her ovens going for Christmas. I normally eat healthy, so my consumption of cookies is limited to tastes of the finished product, so removing them initially was not a problem. And then one day that avoidance came crashing down around me. It was my birthday, and my husband went all out to create a surprise celebration for me and several of my friends. A limo ride to my favorite restaurant in Kansas City. An entire portion of the restaurant was reserved just for us. The finale was a gorgeous cake, my birthday cake, being hoisted by a proud waiter. It was a beautiful, heavily frosted, work of art. I knew that I wanted it. I also knew that I had not informed my husband of my suspicions of having wheat/gluten intolerance. Everyone else was digging into my cake and loving it. So to not hurt feelings, to "fit in" and most important, to feel "normal", I took a small slice I had a couple of bites, and it really was wonderful. I figured I had enough to taste but not enough to create discomfort. I was unfortunately not that lucky.

For those of you who suffer from Celiac disease, lactose intolerance, or any other food that falls under the category of intolerance or sensitivity (allergies can be serious but often affect people differently than an intolerance) you are all too familiar with stomach pain so bad you feel you have been poisoned, spasms in the GI tract that have you convinced an alien being is about to break out of your body and rip you in half, and/or intestinal issues so severe you promise yourself you will never eat anything ever again, you know what my next 16 hours of life were like. It was a day I would never want to redo again. Not only was I feeling horrible, on my birthday with this great party in progress, but I never wanted to have to feel that I had to avoid enjoying some of life's culinary pleasures because of my fussy tummy. I had enough of that my entire childhood, and I was not about to spend my adult life as a "baby who never outgrew colic" as my mother put it. At the very least, I wanted to be able to have a slice of cake on my birthday, apple pie on Thanksgiving, and a Christmas cookie. Most of the time, I eat so healthy I scare people. My love of green vegetables and my declaration of being a "vegeholic" on Facebook and other blogs are what I am known for these days. However, there are days when I want to end my yummy cabbage in sauce dinner with a cookie or two with some almond milk. Store bought ones are a gamble. Some are good, others are so bad I think the packaging would be more tasty. But no store bought item, regardless of how good it is, can substitute for the experience that only your own baking can bring. There is something to the smell of warm cinnamon rolls rising in the oven, its aroma wafting through the kitchen that cannot be replaced by eating a bowl of gluten-free vegan oatmeal with a sprinkle of cinnamon and maple syrup.

I ran into similar issues when it came to pasta. As an Italian who became vegetarian at age 17 because I simply felt better not eating meat, many of my dinners were pasta based. In my pre-dairy allergy days, some combination of wheat and cheese was in just about every meal I ate. Perhaps it was that over-consumption of wheat and dairy that triggered things, but I could no longer eat the way I wanted to, and I also knew that after all this time I did not want to return to my meat eating days, as that felt wrong in my body as well. I could reduce my sweets. While yummy, no one really needs to eat cookies, regardless of what their ingredients are. But I needed real food to eat every day, and I was not ready to subsist on fruit and nuts. I wanted hot fresh foods that I could eat and feed to other people.

As a certified holistic health practitioner with a PhD in my field, I have immense training in dietary wellness, nutrition, how allergies and intolerances can diminish health, and numerous methods including fasting, detoxification, supplementation, and herbal recipes galore to assist in achieving wholeness and recovery. What my 10+ years of training failed to share with me was one single recipe for those who suffer from any of these conditions. The only official remedy I could suggest to my clients was abstinence. Just as diets do not work because of the limits and deprivation they usually employ, health via abstinence is not always easy, even for those who get immensely sick from a bite of a brownie. What was needed was not only awareness of these conditions, but also a viable option so they did not feel they were missing out. It was at that moment, while friends were gleefully celebrating my birthday, when my work took a whole new turn. My mission would be to create treats that were just as good, if not better, than the goodies I had been known for. While I did not realize it then, it was on that day, October 4, 2001 that the New Dawn Kitchen officially began.

In time, I devised recipes that I shared with local clients during holistic coaching sessions. (My practice is primarily focused on assisting those identify hidden causes of excess weight and decreased energy.) Not only were they enjoying the snack samples, but they wanted the recipes themselves. They also wanted more than just cake, such as pasta and their comfort foods back, so back to the kitchen I went. When my clients were no longer sabotaging their gluten/wheat-free diets, they began to really feel and look better. Their children and partners ate meals with them, most without ever suspecting a thing. At the encouragement of friends and clients, I share this book with all of you who need to follow a restricted diet. Yes, you can have your cake and eat it too, and bread and pancakes and donuts and waffles and all sorts of otherwise off-limits foods.

What is Gluten?

Gluten is the protein that naturally occurs in the following grains: wheat, rye, barley, durum, semolina, einkorn, graham, bulgur, couscous, spelt, farro, kamut, and triticale. Commercial oats also contain gluten due to cross contamination in processing, but actually are gluten-free otherwise. Depending on your level of sensitivity will depend if you can use regular oats or if you need to invest in oats that specifically indicate they are gluten-free. I myself am not sensitive enough for the cross-contamination of oats, so I buy regular oats, which are more affordable and certainly easier to obtain. I would consult with your healthcare provider or nutritionist as to whether or not you can handle oats, or any product for that matter, that is processed on equipment or manufactured in the same environment, as a gluten product.

Therefore, gluten will be present in these grains flours and byproducts, such as barley malt, beer, and many flavorings and spices. When in doubt, obtain vanilla, spices, and any food product that says gluten-free, as gluten is in many products you may not expect it to be, for example, cooking spices. Read everything.

What Grains and Flours are Gluten-Free?

Corn flour, cornmeal, and cornstarch
Buckwheat and buckwheat flour
Rice flour- white and brown
Quinoa, quinoa cereal flakes, and quinoa flour
Millet and millet flour
Sorghum flour
Amaranth and amaranth flour
Certified gluten-free oats and oatmeal
Coconut flour
Teff flour
Nut meals and flours- almond, chestnut, pecan, cashew
Garbanzo, fava bean, pea, soy and other bean flours
Tapioca pearls and tapioca starch/flour (they are the same product)
Potato starch
Potato flour (which is different than potato starch)
Sweet potato and yam flour
Arrowroot starch

More about Gluten-Free Flours

Since gluten-free flours are composed of different grains, they will have different textures. This is why it's best to blend and create your own mixes. In many of the cookie and dessert recipes here and in my previous book, ***Gluten-Free, Vegan, and Easily Sugar-Free Desserts,*** I use gluten-free all purpose blend or a variety of gluten-free flours and starches for the best texture. I most frequently use sorghum, garbanzo, and white or brown rice flours, along with one or more starches, to create my own all purpose blend, which I will share later on. While you are already thinking that this is a whole lot to think of when you get that urge to make a batch of cookies, think again. Once you gather your ingredients, you can blend up mixes in large batches and freeze or refrigerate.

When it comes to any of the starches, you can substitute any of them interchangeably, but you may find that you have a taste preference to one over the other. I prefer cornstarch in desserts only because it is the easiest and most affordable, but when making a loaf of bread, I prefer potato starch.

Guar or xanthan gum, a necessary binding agent for gluten-free success, are also interchangeable. You may find guar gum more affordable, but may have to mail order it. Usually a teaspoon per cup of flour is all that is needed. Some recipes can forgo gum, but most will crumble beyond measure. When converting your own recipes, trial and error will be the best guide.

New Dawn Kitchen's Gluten-Free All-Purpose Blend

(Makes 6 cups)
2 cups sorghum flour
1 cup garbanzo flour
1/2 cup coconut flour or almond meal flour
1/2 cup oat or quinoa flour
1 cup cornstarch
1 cup tapioca starch/flour

Why Eat Wheat/Gluten-Free?

There is a growing awareness that a number of individuals experience mild to severe gastro-intestinal distress when eating wheat/gluten containing foods. While most individuals are more likely to have sensitivity to these foods if eaten in excess, there are those who have allergies to wheat or gluten and therefore cannot safely eat even a small portion of the culprit food.
Another concern is Celiac Disease, a condition in which a person is intolerant to gluten containing foods. In the body of someone with this condition, consuming gluten containing food sets off an

autoimmune response that causes damage to the small intestine. This, in turn, causes the small intestine to lose the ability to absorb nutrients, leading to malnutrition, permanent intestinal damage, and possibility of requiring surgery.

There is a belief that removing gluten as well as casein, a protein found in dairy, helps children with Autism Spectrum Disorder. Some parents report improvements in autism symptoms with this dietary regimen. Little actual research has been done, however, on the gluten-free/casein-free diet for autism. However, since there is no dietary need for gluten or casein in the diet, so there is no harm in removing them if they help you or your child's health.

For those who find that eating wheat and/or gluten containing foods creates mild to moderate distress, it is recommended to follow an elimination diet and consult with a healthcare provider and/or dietician for further assistance. In my situation, my gluten intolerance is seasonal, spanning the winter months, whereas my egg yolk and dairy allergies are constant. If you approach your body with awareness, you will know what to do.

Dairy Products: To Eat Or Not To Eat

While most of us are familiar with lactose intolerance and milk allergies, there are other reasons why more and more individuals are reducing or eliminating dairy from their diets. In this age of environmental awareness, using plant-based milk substitutes is more popular due to their smaller impact on environmental waste. Also, for those who are concerned about animal cruelty, avoiding milk helps reduce factory farming practices. Since most dairy cows are supplied with antibiotics, hormones, and fed food that is laced with pesticides, it may be best if we all took a step away from dairy.

For those of you who are vegan (choose to eliminate all animal products), dairy allergic, or lactose intolerant, follow the recipes using whatever milk substitute you wish. You will also find that many of the recipes call for yogurt, cheese, and/or sour cream. For convenience I will call these "milk product", "vegan sour cream", and "non-dairy yogurt " and "vegan cheddar" the first time, and from there, just yogurt, milk, etc. If you bought this book because of your gluten/wheat sensitivity and are not following a dairy-free guideline, feel free to use whatever dairy products you wish in equal measure.

I want to take a moment to discuss the flavor of non-dairy products. If you are very new to dairy alternatives, please note that not all dairy-free milks, cheeses, and other products taste the same. While most would say that they could not tell the difference between one brand of 2% milk from another, I assure you there is major variety in texture, flavor, sweetness, etc between rice and soy milk, and even among the individual brands of soy milk. Be patient, try many brands, and stick with what you love. For me, I really had a hard time with the vegan cheeses, as casein, a common ingredient in dairy-free cheeses, is actually a milk protein, and hence, not dairy-free. The first time I discovered this, I shot out a nasty email to a company, claiming they were falsely advertising their soy cheese, and that if I had wanted dairy, I would have saved $3 and bought real cheese. They apologized, and a week later, a drop shipment of numerous bags of their assorted shredded cheeses were on my doorstep. At first I was really angry, as I made it clear that I am so sensitive to dairy that I get high fevers (105°F) and often need hospitalization if I had more than an accidental taste. I had just recovered from such an episode that luckily I was able to heal from at home, and I felt this really showed their inability to understand that dairy means anything that comes from milk from an animal. Lactose and casein and whey are all different dairy by-products and you can be highly allergic to casein and not be lactose intolerant.

So I stayed away from all cheese, even the truly vegan ones because those that did not have casein tasted like slippery plastic. And then one day I found Daiya cheese online, and my ability to cook and eat my favorite mac and cheese, lasagna, and everything else was restored. Even my husband will eat Daiya cheese. I made a pot of my macaroni and cheese for the 4th of July and those that ate it did not know. I actually took it to be a major compliment when my sister-in-law said it "tasted like Velveeta" because until now, there was no vegan cheese that could fool the taste buds.

I must stress that I am not affiliated with any of the brands I should mention in these pages, but in some cases, like Daiya and Mimic Crème, there was no other alternative (in my opinion) that even came close, and until their emergence, that chapter of my cooking experience was closed.

Fats: The Good, The Bad, And The Ugly

Remember when margarine first came out and we thought it was healthful to smear gobs of it on our food to get the healthful polyunsaturated fats? Well, like most other food trends, the good and the bad fats list keeps getting updated. Here is my take on fats, as far as this cookbook is concerned: use what is readily available to you. While I am the first to say NO to traditional shortening and lard, if you prefer these, then use them. True they are bad for you, but let's be honest- unless you have an extreme food problem, even the most rich and decadent meal eaten in moderation and not on a daily basis should be fine for your health and your waistline. However, I am the first to say that I love good food, and overindulged a few too many times in the writing of this book.

The main fat most of us need to substitute in dairy-free and vegan cooking is butter. Butter in many ways may actually be healthier than the trans fats in most margarines, but for those who cannot or will not have dairy, both products are likely unsafe to use. My suggestion for recipes that really need a "stick" of butter is to use vegan brands such as "Earth Balance". The buttery blend one is quite tasty on gluten-free toast, but again, fat is fat, so a little goes a long way.

The newest “fat” to get attention these days is coconut oil. Coconut oil is reported to have antibiotic and even weight loss benefits when used moderately. Use common sense. Some brands are pricier than others, but I have learned that the higher the price, usually the better the buttery flavor. The lower priced ones in general smell and taste like coconut, so keep this in mind. Some cookie recipes taste wonderful with this coconut flavor, whereas other recipes it is just too overpowering, so a higher grade of coconut oil is needed. However, even the lower cost coconut oil can be more than seven dollars for a jar that is smaller than a jar of spaghetti sauce and you might wind up using the whole thing, if not more, for one recipe.

Therefore when I bake cakes and prepare recipes that require a lot of oil, I rely on either canola or extra light olive oil. If you prefer another oil besides olive or canola oil, simply substitute that oil for the butter or oil called for in a recipe. I especially like coconut oil is Asian recipes.

Need To Reduce Fat?

While our recipes will be naturally cholesterol-free because we have omitted all animal products, almost all of our recipes contain oil, margarine, cheese, or all. However, most are not considered low-fat. For those of you who need or want to reduce the fat, there are a number of substitutions you can use.

One of the most popular is to use less oil and more water to sauté in. For baking, applesauce works well in baking recipes, as does pumpkin, mashed sweet potato, or any gluten-free pureed fruit or baby food. If you are already using one of these for your egg replacement, be careful not to add too much, or your recipe will be too wet. My overall suggestion is to use less cooking oil, less oil in dressings, and more broth, vinegar, water, or non-fat liquids whenever possible. You can also go lighter on the cheese, sour cream, etc. I would prefer to just eat a smaller portion of something cheesy and higher in fat, like lasagna, and then fill up on a low fat salad or soup as more of the main dish on those days.

Egg-Free Cooking

If you are vegan or cannot consume eggs or egg yolks like me, you have several options to use as substitutes. Unlike swapping oils and milk for another product, not every egg substitute will work for every recipe, so removing eggs from a recipe is perhaps just as tricky, if not more so, than making the gluten-free switch. My experience is that if you have a recipe that uses 3 or more eggs, you will find it harder to have successful results with an egg substitute. However, it can be done if you take the time to experiment with which product mimics the best texture for your recipe. Most of my recipes will use a product called Ener-G Egg Replacer, which I refer to as egg replacer. In baking, which this cookbook does not really explore (see my other book The New Dawn Kitchen: Gluten-Free, Vegan, and Easily Sugar-Free Desserts) you will see other options, such as tofu or flaxseed meal with water. Do your research and use what you are most comfortable using for your egg replacement. Those who eat eggs can use real eggs/egg whites for the number of egg replacer portions I mention.

Want To Reduce Sugar?

In standard recipes, agave nectar, maple syrup, or any liquid sweetener that is gluten-free will work fine. Barley Malt is not gluten-free, but often sits on store shelves immediately next to rice syrup, which is. When substituting a liquid sweetener for granulated in your own recipes, reduce liquid in recipe by ¼ cup. I am very sugar sensitive, so for my own baking, I use artificial sweetener and/or sugar-free maple syrup, then use 1/3 of the sugar called for in the recipe. While artificial sweeteners are not healthful in the least, this is one of those choices I need to make. I use stevia for granulated sweetening and sugar-free maple syrup mixed with a bit of rice syrup for my liquid sweetening. While maple syrup, rice syrup and agave nectar are more healthful choices, they still have a sugar content that spike my blood sugar if I have more than a couple of bites. I actually prefer rice syrup and use it sparingly as a caramel sauce substitute on rice cream.

Honey is an animal product and is not in theory truly vegan, but locally gathered honey has loads of health benefits, especially for allergy sufferers. I often take a spoonful of honey all winter long to help offset my seasonal allergies. It's just a spoonful, but I find it's like a natural vaccine for me. I also realize this makes me less-than vegan, and I call myself "vegan-enough". Make conscious choices with what you put in your body, as you are the one who has to answer for your health and well-being.

Ultimately the choice is yours when it comes to sweetening your goods. Remember when using a liquid sweetener, use less than the amount of sugar called for unless my recipe already calls for a liquid sweetener (taste test to adjust sweetness level). Adjust the liquid by two tablespoons less to begin with.

Substitutes For Cream And Condensed Milk Products

Recently I discovered a groovy product named Mimic Crème that works for those of us who need a gluten-free vegan cream product. It is on the grocery shelf in one of those aseptic containers that soymilk comes in, but refrigerate after opening. I make the most awesome Italian food such as Alfredo with this, but you can use plain soy or rice milk instead. It's not much higher in fat than either option, but may be harder to locate. I would say Mimic Crème goes into that same category as Daiya cheese- offering gluten-free vegan freedom for those of us who must abstain from the traditional, and as such, all sorts of recipes, such as a good cup of coffee, is back in my life.

Peanut Free/Nut Free

For a nut-free peanut butter substitute try using sunflower seed butter, commonly found as the product "Sunbutter" in recipes. Sesame seed butter (also called tahini) is another choice, but requires (in my opinion) a touch of liquid sweetener to offset its savory taste. Other seed and nut butters include macadamia nut butter, cashew butter, pecan butter, and my favorite, almond butter. You may want to sweetener or salt the recipe differently depending on your like for salt and sweet. You can also use soynuts in recipes or for snacks in equal measure as you would use other nuts.

Salt-Free

There are a number of potassium salt products out there for those who must watch their sodium intake. All are fine, but please do not use an herbal blend like Mrs. Dash for baking! Feel free to use in equal measure or less, as potassium salt, as far as I am concerned, seems more salty and concentrated.

Appetizers

Vegan Mozzarella Sticks

These really hit the spot, especially with hearty, chunky tomato sauce.

1 8oz block of vegan Mozzarella (I use Follow Your Heart)
oil for frying

Wet Ingredients

½ cup gluten-free all-purpose flour
½ cup water
1 tablespoon cornmeal
1 tablespoon cornstarch
salt, oregano, pepper, garlic powder, and other desired spices to taste

Dry Ingredients

1 cup gluten-free breadcrumbs
½ teaspoon salt
½ teaspoon parsley flakes
½ teaspoon black pepper
½ teaspoon garlic powder
¼ teaspoon onion powder
¼ teaspoon oregano
¼ teaspoon basil

Combine ingredients for wet mix. The consistency should be like pancake batter, so adjust accordingly if needed. In another bowl, stir together breadcrumbs and remaining spices. Remove vegan cheese from refrigerator and slice into ½" strips.

Lightly coat each stick with flour. Dredge each stick in the wet mix, then toss in bread crumbs until fully coated. Place sticks on a cookie sheet in a single layer, not touching one another, and freeze for at least one hour.

Heat up your deep fryer, or if you don't have one, pour an inch of (safflower or peanut have the highest heat tolerance) oil into the bottom of a deep skillet or deep fryer and heat.

Carefully dip the end of a stick into the oil to check for readiness; if the oil sizzles continually, it's ready. If not, let it heat up some more. Once it's up to temperature, fry sticks in small batches so they do not crowd the pan and reduce the oil's heat too much. Fry about 1 minute per side, or until they're golden brown and you can see a little cheese oozing through the breadcrumbs. Serve with marinara sauce for dipping.

Garlic Bruschetta

1 pound tomatoes, diced

2 cloves garlic, minced

1 tablespoon minced fresh parsley

1 tablespoon chopped basil

2 tablespoon balsamic vinegar

¼ cup olive oil

1 baguette, sliced, our recipe or any gluten-free bread of choice

Oil to coat the bread

Vegan Parmesan cheese (optional)

Combine the tomatoes, garlic, parsley, basil, vinegar, and oil, and let marinate for at least 30 minutes.

Preheat oven to 400°F. Brush the sliced bread with olive oil on both sides and place on a baking sheet. Bake for just a few minutes, until bread is lightly toasted. Top each slice of bread with a spoonful of the tomato mixture, and sprinkle with vegan Parmesan cheese if desired.

Italian Rice Balls

Whether as an appetizer or even as a meatball substitute, these little things are jam packed with flavor.

2 cups cooked hot cooked rice

¾ cup shredded vegan cheddar cheese

1 egg replacer portion, prepared according to instructions

Salt and black pepper, to taste

Pinch of onion powder or flakes

1 ½ teaspoons of mustard

1 cup corn gluten-free tortilla crumbs or gluten-free cornflake crumbs

2 teaspoons of paprika

Combine all ingredients except crumbs and paprika. Chill for at least one hour. Form into small balls using 1 tablespoon mixture for each.

Blend crumbs and paprika. Roll balls in crumbs until well coated. Heat oil in a large skillet or deep fryer to 375°F. Fry in small batches about 3 minutes. Drain. Serve with optional marinara or other desired dipping sauces.

Stuffed Mushrooms

These mushrooms are easily enjoyed by those who are not gluten-free or vegan, and are a great appetizer for a party or Thanksgiving.

15 - 20 button mushrooms

1 small zucchini, diced

½ cup finely chopped onion

1 piece of gluten-free bread, cubed

¼ cup finely chopped cashews or other nuts

1 teaspoon vegan parmasan cheese

½ teaspoon salt

¼ teaspoon garlic powder

4 tablespoons vegan butter

Preheat oven to 350˚F. Wash mushrooms carefully to remove all dirt, and remove stems. Melt butter and add other ingredients and stir to create a stuffing. Spoon stuffing into mushroom cavities

Bake uncovered for 15 minutes, until browned. Serve immediately.

Stuffed Tomatoes

A great light meal or yummy appetizer.

4 large firm tomatoes

2 tablespoons of olive oil

½ cup red onion, diced small

2 cups cooked rice

¼ teaspoon of oregano

Salt and pepper to taste

Preheat oven to 350°F. Cut ½ inch off the top of each of tomato. Use a small knife or a melon baller to gently scoop out the insides of the tomatoes, being careful not to cut through the bottoms.

Sauté the onions for a few minutes in olive oil, until soft.

In a large bowl, combine the remaining ingredients. Using a small spoon, scoop the rice mixture and stuff each tomato. Gently pack in the rice, so the whole tomato is full.

Lightly brush the tomatoes with a bit olive oil and place in a baking dish. Bake for 25 minutes, or until the tomatoes are soft and begin to shrivel. Do not over bake.

Artichoke Appetizer

Artichokes are an underrated super food. Enjoy these anytime.

2 cans (14 oz) artichoke hearts, or 2 packages (10 oz) frozen
1 clove garlic, minced
¼ cup olive oil
2 teaspoons of lemon juice
¼ teaspoon white or black pepper
¼ cup oregano

Drain and quarter the artichokes.

Combine the rest of the ingredients, making a dressing, and pour over the artichoke hearts.

Marinate for at least 1 hour. Serve as a salad topping, on pasta, or as part of an array of appetizers.

Polenta Rounds

2 cups milk product
1 quart vegetable stock
2 tablespoons vegan butter
3 cups dry polenta
3 cups mashed tofu
2 cups shredded vegan Mozzarella cheese
1 cup vegan Parmesan cheese
1 egg replacer, prepared according to package instructions
¼ cup chopped parsley, fresh preferred
Salt and pepper to taste
Oil, for brushing
Additional Parmesan, Mozzarella, sauce, or other items for toppings

In a large saucepan, combine milk, stock, and butter and bring to boil. Slowly stir in polenta, reduce heat to medium-low, and continue cooking, and stirring, until polenta pulls from edge of pan. It will resemble the texture of cooked hot cereal.

Pour half of the cooked polenta into a greased 9x13 baking pan. In a bowl, add mashed tofu, cheeses, prepared egg replacer, and parsley. Mix well and evenly spread over polenta, then top with remaining polenta. Refrigerate at least 30 minutes.

Preheat oven to broil. Turn cooled polenta onto a cookie sheet. Using a 2 inch round cookie cutter, cut circles from cooled polenta. Brush each round with oil on each side and broil on each side on the center oven rack, for 6 minutes, or until browned, being careful not to burn.

When done, blot with paper towel to remove any excess oil. Sprinkle rounds with Parmesan cheese, sauce, or any other toppings of choice.

Veggie Antipasti

Certainly not the traditional style, but I really enjoy this version.

½ cup balsamic vinegar
½ cup olive oil
½ cup lemon juice
2 tablespoons sweetener of choice
2 tablespoons fresh basil
1 broccoli crown, cut into small florets
1 green pepper, cut into matchsticks
1 red pepper, cut into matchsticks
½ cup mushrooms,
½ cup chopped celery
1 cup green and/or black olives, sliced

Add 1 cup water in a large saucepan or skillet. Add broccoli, peppers, mushrooms, and celery and bring to a boil. Reduce heat and simmer, covered for 2 minutes, just enough to blanche but not boil and overly cook the vegetables.

Prepare the dressing by combining the vinegar, oil, lemon juice, sweetener, and basil. Pour over the vegetables, add the olives, and let marinate overnight.

Italian Roasted Tomato Salsa

5 large ripe tomatoes, sliced in half
4 cloves of minced garlic
¼ cup fresh parsley
¼ cup olive oil
Salt and pepper, to taste
2 sliced gluten-free baguettes or other desired bread product

Cover bottom of a medium baking dish with a layer of tomatoes. Sprinkle with crushed garlic, salt, pepper, and parsley, then drizzle with olive oil.

Continue layering until remaining ingredients are gone. Roast, uncovered, in oven on low heat, about 2 hours.

Serve with sliced baguettes as an appetizer.

Panini

Panini is the Italian word for sandwich.

½ cup red wine vinegar
4 cloves garlic, peeled and minced
2 teaspoon dried oregano
¼ cup olive oil
2/3 cup pitted chopped green olives
2/3 cup pitted, chopped Kalamata olives
½ cup chopped roasted red peppers
Salt and pepper to taste
1 large loaf gluten-free Ciabatta bread, about 18 inches long
1 red onion, sliced into thin rings
2 cups baby spinach or other greens
Vegan Parmesan, or other cheese, optional

Whisk first 3 ingredients in a large bowl to blend. Gradually blend in olive oil. Stir in olives and roasted red peppers. Season to taste with salt and pepper.

Cut ciabatta in half horizontally. Pull out all but 1 inch of bread from inside of each half to create a cavity. Spread olive mixture evenly onto both sides of loaf and set top half aside. Working with bottom half, top olive mixture with even layers of red onion rings and red peppers, followed by a layer of spinach or greens. Sprinkle with optional cheese.

Carefully place top half of loaf on top and wrap sandwich tightly with plastic wrap to compress. Let it sit for several hours, refrigerated to allow flavors to blend. When ready to serve, unwrap sandwich and, using a large serrated knife, cut sandwich into pieces by slicing it crosswise into 1 ½ inch thick slices and then cutting each of these sections in half to form individual portions. Secure each portion with a toothpick.

Baked Zucchini Sticks

So much better for you, and in my opinion, tastier.

4 medium zucchini, peeled and sliced into matchsticks

2 cups gluten-free breadcrumbs, seasoned to taste

2 egg replacer portions, prepared according to instructions

2 tablespoons of water

Cut each zucchini in half widthwise, then cut each half lengthwise into quarters. In a shallow bowl, combine bread crumbs and spices.

In another bowl, beat egg and water. Dip zucchini in egg replacer mixture, then coat with crumb mixture. Coat again in egg mixture and crumbs.

Arrange on a baking sheet coated with nonstick cooking spray. Bake at 375° F for 20-25 minutes or until tender and golden, turning once about halfway through.

Veggie Boats

You can use either yellow or green squash, or small eggplants, or a combination of all three, with equally delicious results.

6 medium zucchini ***or*** yellow squash ***or*** 3 small eggplants

2 cups gluten-free breadcrumbs, seasoned to taste

2 egg replacer portions, prepared according to instructions

1 large tomato, diced

½ cup vegan Parmesan cheese

¼ cup minced fresh parsley

2 garlic cloves, minced

½ cup vegetable broth

Salt and pepper to taste

2 tablespoons vegan butter, melted

Cut vegetables in half lengthwise. With a spoon, scoop out and reserve pulp, leaving 3/8-in. shell. Cook shells in salted water for 2 minutes; remove and drain. Chop pulp; place in a bowl. Add the bread crumbs, eggs replacer, tomato, Parmesan cheese, parsley and garlic. Stir in broth, salt and pepper. Stuff into shells.

Place in a greased 9x13 baking dish. Drizzle with melted butter. Bake, uncovered, at 350° F for 20 minutes or until golden brown.

Soups and Salads

Minestrone

This is reprinted from my ***Virtuous Vegan*** book. Growing up Italian in a heavily Italian town, I had my share of delicious Minestrone. That was years ago, and while I am not sure I would remember it if I tasted it, I am very pleased with how this one came out.

2 tablespoons olive oil

1 clove of garlic, chopped

2 medium onions, chopped

2 cups chopped celery

3carrots, sliced

4 cups vegetable broth

4 cups tomato sauce

1 cup canned kidney beans, drained

3 zucchini, diced

1 teaspoon each dried oregano and basil

Salt and pepper to taste

½ cup gluten-free small shells or other pasta

In a large stock pot, over medium-low heat, sauté onions, celery, carrots, and garlic for 5 minutes. Add broth, water, and tomato sauce, bring to boil, stirring frequently. Reduce heat to low and add remaining ingredients. Once pasta is cooked the soup is done.

Veggie Pizza Soup

A really great way to get your children to enjoy vegetables.

1 cup fresh sliced mushrooms

1 small red onion, diced

1 teaspoon vegetable oil

2 cups water

15 ounce jar of pizza sauce

1 green pepper, diced

1 cup chopped tomatoes

½ cup sliced black olives

¼ teaspoon Italian seasoning

¼ cup each vegan Parmesan and Mozzarella cheeses

In a large saucepan, heat oil over medium heat. Sauté mushrooms and onion in oil for 2 to 3 minutes, or until tender. Mix in water, pizza sauce, tomatoes, olives, and Italian seasoning. Cover, and bring to a boil. Reduce heat; cover, and simmer for 20 minutes, stirring occasionally. Before serving, stir in Parmesan cheese. Garnish with Mozzarella cheese.

Vegan Wedding Soup

No sausage or meatballs in here, and you will not miss them!

2 tablespoons grated Parmesan cheese

1 teaspoon dried basil

3 tablespoons minced onion

2 ½ quarts vegetable broth

2 cups spinach

1 cup small shell or other gluten-free pasta

¾ cup diced carrots

1 recipe Cheese Rice Balls

In a large stockpot heat broth to boiling; stir in the spinach, pasta, carrot and onion. Return to boil; reduce heat to medium. Cook, stirring frequently, at a slow boil for 10 minutes or until pasta is al dente.

Serve hot with Parmesan cheese and rice balls added immediately before serving.

Tomato Lentil Soup

1 cup dry lentils

1 ¼ quarts water, divided

¾ cup uncooked long grain white rice

1 tablespoon vegetable oil

2 cloves garlic, minced

1 tablespoon chopped fresh parsley

Salt and black pepper, to taste

1 quart tomato sauce

¼ cup vegan Parmesan cheese for topping

Place lentils in a pot with 3 cups water. Bring to a boil, reduce heat to low, and cook 20 minutes or until tender. Drain and set aside.

Bring rice and 1 1/3 cup water to boil in a pot. Reduce heat, cover, and simmer for 20 minutes.

In a large pot, bring the tomato sauce and 4 cups water to a boil. Mix in cooked lentils and rice. Return to a boil, reduce heat to medium-low, and simmer for 30 minutes. Sprinkle with Parmesan cheese to serve.

Italian House Salad

Everyone's house salad is different, and so I do my best to get everyone's version when I go out to eat.

1 large head romaine lettuce, rinsed, dried, and torn

1 large head red leaf lettuce, rinsed, dried, and torn

1 (14 ounce) can artichoke hearts, drained and quartered

1 cup sliced red onion

1/3 cup oil

1 cup balsamic vinegar

¼ teaspoon ground black pepper

1/3 cup vegan Parmesan cheese

½ cup chick peas

¼ cup black olives

Dash of salt, pepper, and oregano

In a large bowl, combine the romaine lettuce, red leaf lettuce, artichoke hearts, and red onions. Toss together.

Prepare the dressing by whisking together the olive oil, vinegar, salt, pepper, oregano, and cheese. Refrigerate until chilled and pour over salad to coat. Toss and serve.

Tomato Basil Salad

Growing up in the Garden State, really large ripe tomatoes were easy to come by. As such, I became very creative with tomatoes.

4 large ripe red tomatoes, sliced

1 cup artichoke hearts, rinsed and drained

10 fresh basil leaves, chopped

½ cup red onion, sliced into thin rings

10 Kalamata olives

¼ cup olive oil

½ cup balsamic vinegar

Salt and pepper to taste

½ teaspoon dried oregano

¼ cup vegan Parmesan cheese

¼ cup marinated red peppers, cut into slices

Alternate and overlap the tomato slices, artichokes, and onion slices on a platter. Sprinkle the basil over the top. Scatter the olives over the salad. Prepare dressing by combining the oil and vinegar, and season with salt, pepper, and oregano. Allow to sit at room temperature 15 minutes before serving. Top with olives, peppers, and Parmesan before serving.

Italian Potato Salad

As a child, I never liked mayonnaise, and believe I was better off for it. Even today, with many vegan blends available, I still avoid mayo. Bring this to your next BBQ or gathering, and everyone will ask for the recipe.

5 large Yukon Gold potatoes

5 stalks celery, chopped

1 large red onion, chopped

1 cup green olives, chopped

¼ cup olive oil

½ cup balsamic vinegar

¼ teaspoon garlic powder

Salt, black pepper, and oregano to taste

Place potatoes in a large saucepan, cover with water, and bring to a boil. Reduce the heat to medium-low, and simmer until the potatoes are tender, about 15 minutes. Drain and cool, then cut into 1 inch cubes.

Combine the potatoes, celery, onion, and olives in a large bowl. Whisk together the olive oil, red wine vinegar, and garlic powder in a small bowl. Pour the dressing over the potatoes and vegetables; mix well. Season, then chill. Stir before serving.

Pasta salad

1 (16 ounce) package gluten-free Rotini pasta

1 cup Italian-style salad dressing

1 cup vegan Caesar salad, or other creamy vegan dressing

1 cup vegan Parmesan cheese

1 red bell pepper, diced

1 green bell pepper, chopped

1 red onion, diced

In a large pot of salted boiling water, cook pasta until al dente, rinse under cold water and drain.

In a large bowl, combine the pasta, Italian salad dressing, Caesar dressing, red bell pepper, green bell pepper and red onion. Mix well and serve chilled or at room temperature.

Eggplant Salad

3 medium eggplants

1 clove garlic, crushed

3 tablespoons olive oil

1 tablespoon balsamic vinegar

2 tablespoons granulated sweetener

1 teaspoon dried parsley

1 teaspoon dried oregano

¼ teaspoon dried basil

Salt and pepper to taste

Preheat the oven to 350° F. Puncture eggplants with a fork, and place on a baking sheet. Bake for 1 ½ hours, or until soft, turning occasionally. Cool, then peel and dice.

In a large bowl, stir together the garlic, olive oil, vinegar, sugar, parsley, oregano, basil, salt and pepper. Add the diced eggplant, and stir to coat. Refrigerate for at least 2 hours before serving to marinate.

Italian Melon Salad

This is a great light meal on a hot day, as well as an equally enjoyable dessert.

2 cups chilled and seeded watermelon balls

2 cups chilled and seeded cantaloupe balls

¼ cup agave nectar or other liquid sweetener

1 tablespoon of raspberry ***or*** balsamic vinegar

½ cup fresh raspberries

Fresh mint, as optional garnish

Divide chilled watermelon and cantaloupe among 4 bowls.

Stir together agave nectar and vinegar and drizzle some over each serving. Top with raspberries. Garnish with fresh mint sprigs if desired.

Bread Salad

The first time I had this, I was blown away. Now, with my gluten-free and vegan version, it's everything I remember it to be.

1 loaf crusty gluten-free bread, cut into one inch cubes
2 zucchinis, peeled, seeded, and diced
1 dozen cherry or grape tomatoes, diced
¼ cup red onion, diced
¼ cup sliced black olives, drained
¼ cup sliced green olives, drained
1 bunch fresh basil, coarsely chopped
½ cup marinated red peppers
½ cup marinated artichokes
½ cup garbanzo beans, rinsed and drained
½ cup red wine vinegar
¼ cup vegan Parmesan cheese

Allow bread cubes to sit overnight on baking sheet.

In a large salad bowl combine bread cubes with zucchini, tomatoes, onion, olives, and basil and set aside.

Place marinated peppers and artichokes in mixing bowl and whisk in vinegar. Add beans. Pour over salad and toss gently. Allow to stand for 30 minutes in refrigerator. Right before serving, add Parmesan to salad and mix gently.

White Kidney Bean Soup

1 white onion, diced
1 tablespoon of olive oil
2 garlic cloves, finely minced
2 cans of white kidney beans, drained and rinsed
1(14 oz) can diced tomatoes
1 quart of vegetable broth
2 tablespoons of dried oregano
2 tablespoons of dried basil
Salt and pepper to taste
2 cups of spinach or other leafy greens

In a large stock pot, add olive oil and onion; cook 4-5 minutes; add all additional ingredients other than spinach/greens.

Cook on medium-low for 30 minutes. Add spinach/greens, and simmer 1-2 minutes, just until wilted.

Breads

Parmesan Breadsticks

This recipe is my favorite bread and works with just about every meal, from soup to entrees.

½ cup amaranth flour
¾ cup garbanzo flour
1/3 cup tapioca starch
2 tablespoons granulated sweetener
1 single package quick-rise dry yeast
1 teaspoon xanthan gum
½ teaspoon garlic powder
½ teaspoon salt
1 teaspoon olive oil
Melted vegan butter for brushing
½ cup vegan Parmesan, for topping

Mix together all dry ingredients other than melted butter and Parmesan. Stir in oil and ¾ cup warm water at 110°F. Beat dough with electric mixer on high speed 2 minutes, or by hand, until smooth.

Transfer dough to a large plastic bag with 1 corner snipped off to serve as a pastry bag. Squeeze bag to create 12 breadsticks of equal size. Cover and let rise for 30 minutes, or until breadsticks have doubled in size. Brush with melted butter and Parmesan.

Preheat oven to 400°F. Bake 20 minutes, or until dark golden brown all over and crisp on bottom. Serve immediately.

Tomato Focaccia

A thick, seasoned bread that doubles as a pan pizza crust.

Whisk together:

1 cup sorghum flour
1 cup tapioca starch
½ cup potato flour
2 teaspoons xanthan gum
1 ¼ teaspoons sea salt
1 teaspoon dried minced onion
½ teaspoon garlic powder
2 teaspoons dried oregano
2 teaspoons dried basil
1 large tomato, sliced into rings

Prepare in a glass bowl or measuring cup
Add 1 tablespoon active dry yeast:
1 ¼ cups water at 110°F
A pinch of granulated sweetener

When the yeast is ready, pour the mixture into the dry ingredients and add:

4 tablespoons extra virgin olive oil
1 tablespoon agave nectar
Egg replacer for 1 egg prepared according to box instructions

Preheat oven to 350°F. Stir to combine. The dough should be sticky and resemble muffin batter. Dust a round pan with cornmeal and add focaccia. Wet your hand and shape into a rounded loaf. Place the pan into the warm oven and allow it to rise for 20 minutes. Press sliced tomatoes into dough. Bake 25 minutes or until golden.

Garlic Baguette

When I take the time to make this, it's my favorite bread for roast vegetable sandwiches.

2/3 cup sorghum flour
1/3 cup amaranth flour
½ cup millet flour
1 cup tapioca starch
2 teaspoons xanthan gum
1 ¼ teaspoon salt
2 teaspoons dry egg replacer
1 teaspoon garlic powder
1 clove of garlic, minced, as garnish

Prepare the yeast by adding1 tablespoon instant dry yeast or rapid yeast to1 ¼ cups water at 110°F, then add 1 teaspoon of any sweetener, granulated or liquid. Wait 10 minutes for the yeast to proof.

Mix together the yeast mix with 4 tablespoons extra virgin olive oil
3 tablespoons agave nectar
½ teaspoon cider vinegar

Gently combine the dry and liquid ingredients. Knead the dough by either using a bread machine, a kitchen aid, or simply by hand. After 3 minutes, let dough rest 1 hour for rapid yeast and up to 2 hours for regular rise.

Punch down the dough and shape into a baguette. Press minced garlic into top. Allow loaf to rise a second time, about 2 hours. Preheat oven to 350°F. Grease a cookie sheet and place bread in center. Bake 30 minutes. It should sound hollow when done.

Cheesy Dinner Rolls

It's amazing easy these are to make, and how versatile. Make extra and freeze if desired. **Makes 12 rolls**

1 cup brown rice flour
¾ cup tapioca starch
1/3 cup millet flour
2/3 cup sorghum flour
1 tablespoon potato flour
2 tablespoons granulated sweetener
2 teaspoons xanthan gum
1 teaspoon salt
1 package active dry yeast
½ teaspoon sure-jell/fruit pectin (this is vegan, gelatin is not)
¼ teaspoon agar powder
Egg replacer for 2 eggs, prepared according to package instructions
1 ½ cups warm water at 110°F
1 tablespoon vegan sour cream
2 tablespoons oil
½ cup shredded vegan Mozzarella cheese

Heat oven to 200°F for five minutes, then shut off. Spray muffin tin with non-stick spray. Place all dry ingredients other than egg replacer, yeast, sure-jell, and agar powder in a medium bowl and blend well. Place egg replacer, warm water, sour cream, and oil in a bowl and mix until blended. Slowly add dry ingredients. If using a mixer, increase speed to medium for 4 minutes. Gently stir in cheese.

Divide dough into 12 equal portions and place one into each muffin cup. Allow to rise for 20 minutes. When they've risen, remove from oven and preheat oven to 375°F. Place muffin tin back into oven and bake for 20 minutes, until golden.

Sun-Dried Tomato and Olive Loaf

½ cup amaranth flour
½ cup garbanzo flour
½ cup sorghum flour
1/3 cup tapioca starch
2 tablespoons flax seed meal
3 teaspoons xanthan gum
½ cup pitted Kalamata olives, chopped roughly
1 cup sun-dried tomatoes, sliced into thin strips
2 teaspoons active dry yeast
1 teaspoon salt
Egg replacer for 2 eggs, prepared according to instructions
¾ cup water, room temperature
5 tablespoons extra virgin olive oil
2 teaspoons agave nectar
2 teaspoons apple cider vinegar

Preheat the oven to 200°F. Add the flours, yeast, and all other dry ingredients other than salt and vegetables into a medium bowl. Stir in flax meal and combine.

Combine wet ingredients, including the prepared egg replacer, using a hand-mixer or stir by hand. When fully combined, add olives and tomatoes. Slowly add dry ingredient mixture and mix with a wooden spoon until fully blended without lumps.

Grease a loaf pan and pour the dough into the pan. Turn off the oven and place loaf inside. Allow the dough to rise for 90 minutes. It should rise to the very top of the pan.

Increase heat to 350˚F and bake for approximately 40 minutes. The crust should be golden. Allow to cool slightly before removing it from the pan to finish cooling.

Pizza Dough

This is the basis for many other recipes to follow, especially the calzones and strombolis, and what I used on the cover.

In a measuring cup, combine:

1 cup of water at 110°F
1 package dry, active yeast
1 tablespoon granulated sweetener

Whisk together in a bowl and let it sit for 10 minutes or until it begins to foam.

In a large bowl, combine:

2 tablespoons olive oil
1 teaspoon each or dried basil, oregano, garlic, and parsley
2 teaspoons apple cider vinegar
1 teaspoon salt
½ teaspoon xanthan gum

Add to the yeast mixture. Then stir in 2 ½ cups gluten-free all-purpose flour.

Knead dough by hand for a few minutes. Oil a pan and sprinkle cornmeal on it to prevent dough from sticking. Shape dough to desired shape of crust round, square, or mini, and let sit 20 minutes.

Preheat oven to 425°F. Bake the crust for 10 minutes. Remove from oven and add your sauce, vegan cheese, veggies, or any other desired toppings. Return to oven and bake another 10 minutes, or until cheese is melted and hot.

Ciabatta

2/3 cup sorghum flour
1/3 cup amaranth flour
½ cup garbanzo flour
1 cup potato starch
2 teaspoons xanthan gum
1 ¼ teaspoon salt
2 teaspoons dry egg replacer
Melted vegan butter for the top

Prepare the yeast by adding 1tablespoon instant dry yeast or rapid yeast to 1 ¼ cups water at 110°F, then add 1 teaspoon of any sweetener, granulated or liquid. Wait 10 minutes for the yeast to proof.

Mix together the yeast mix with 4 tablespoons extra virgin olive oil
3 tablespoons agave nectar
½ teaspoon cider vinegar

Gently combine the dry and liquid ingredients. Knead the dough by either using a bread machine, a kitchen aid, or simply by hand. After 3 minutes, let dough rest 1 hour for rapid yeast and up to 2 hours for regular rise.

Punch down the dough and shape into a long flat rectangle. Allow loaf to rise a second time, about 2 hours.

Preheat oven to 350°F. Grease a cookie sheet and place bread in center. Brush with melted butter. Bake 30 minutes. It should sound hollow when done.

Calzones

I just love these. Not as cheesy and heavy as the original, but very filling and very much worth the effort.

1 portion of our pizza dough recipe

1 cup pizza sauce

2 cups shredded Mozzarella cheese

2 tablespoons vegan butter, melted

2 cups assorted vegetables of choice such as artichokes, broccoli, spinach, etc.

Roll out dough on a lightly floured surface; shape into a 16 x 10 inch rectangle. Transfer to a lightly greased cookie sheet. Spoon pizza sauce in a stripe down the center of dough lengthwise; add veggies and cheese filling. Make diagonal cuts 1 ½ inches apart down each side, cutting within a ½ inch of the filling. Criss cross strips over filling, sealing with water. Brush top with melted butter.

Bake at 350°F for 35 to 45 minutes. Serve immediately. Serve with optional additional tomato sauce.

Stromboli

Another Italian favorite of mine that I am glad I recreated.

1 portion of our pizza crust recipe

1 (10 ounce) package pizza crust dough

1 green bell pepper, chopped

1 cup fresh spinach leaves

1 red onion, finely chopped

1 (14 ounce) jar pizza sauce

½ cup sliced mushrooms

¼ cup vegan butter, melted

½ cup sliced black olives

1 tomato, sliced into rings

1 cup shredded vegan Mozzarella cheese

Preheat oven to 400° F. In a skillet over medium heat, cook bell pepper, onions, pizza sauce and mushrooms for five minutes. Lay pizza dough flat on cookie sheet. Distribute tomato slices over dough. Place a heaping pile of the sauce mixture on one side of dough (some may be left over). Sprinkle with Mozzarella cheese. Fold dough over and pinch ends and sides together. Poke holes in the top and brush melted butter on it. Cook in a preheated oven for 30 minutes or until golden brown. Slice into individual sections to serve.

Unbeefy Pizza Rolls

I used to use mock ground beef in the past, but since becoming gluten-free and developing my egg and dairy allergies, I have not really found a commercially available ground beef substitute. In many cases, I use lentils. If you can find a gluten-free vegan meat substitute, feel free to use instead, or just omit lentils if they are not calling out to you in this recipe.

1 cup cooked lentils

1 (8 ounce) can tomato sauce

½ cup shredded Mozzarella cheese

½ teaspoon dried oregano

1 portion of our pizza dough recipe

Preheat oven to 375°F. Heat tomato sauce, Mozzarella cheese and oregano over low-medium heat for 5 minutes, or until cheese melts.

Separate dough into eight rectangles, pinching seams together. Place about 3 tablespoons of lentil mixture along one long side of each rectangle. Roll up, jelly-roll style, starting with a long side. Cut each roll into three pieces. Place, seam side down, 2 inches apart on greased baking sheets.

Bake for 15 minutes or until golden brown.

Pasta and Grains

Arrabbiata

This spicy tomato sauce is my favorite to use in most hearty dishes like lasagna or manicotti, as well as a dipping sauce for breadsticks or appetizers.

1 teaspoon olive oil
1 cup chopped onion
4 cloves garlic, minced
2 tablespoons balsamic vinegar
1 tablespoon sweetener of choice, optional
1 (16 ounce) package of gluten-free pasta
¼ cup extra virgin olive oil, divided
2 cloves garlic, minced
2 cups vegetable broth
½ teaspoon garlic powder
1 tablespoon chopped fresh basil
1 teaspoon crushed red pepper flakes
2 tablespoons tomato paste
½ teaspoon Italian seasoning
2 (14.5 ounce) cans peeled and diced tomatoes
2 tablespoons chopped fresh parsley

Cook pasta according to package instructions.

Heat oil in a large skillet or saucepan over medium heat. Sauté onion and garlic in oil for 5 minutes.

Stir in vinegar, sweetener, basil, red pepper, parsley, tomato paste, Italian seasoning, black pepper and tomatoes; bring to a boil. Reduce heat to medium, and simmer uncovered about 15 minutes. Ladle over the hot cooked pasta of your choice.

Pasta with Cauliflower

I prefer to eat as many vegetables as possible, especially when I can add them to a pasta or rice dish. This dish is great with salad and breadsticks.

1 head cauliflower, broken into small florets
½ cup oil
1 onion, chopped
2 cloves garlic, minced
1 teaspoon chopped fresh parsley
¼ teaspoon garlic powder
Salt and pepper to taste
2 tablespoons vegan Parmesan cheese
1 pound gluten-free spaghetti or other long pasta

Cook pasta in a large pot of boiling salted water until al dente. Transfer into a large serving bowl.

Meanwhile, break cauliflower into flowerets, and steam until tender.

Heat oil in a large skillet. Add onion and sauté until golden. Add garlic, and sauté until golden brown. Stir in cauliflower and seasonings.

Toss with onion and cauliflower mixture, and top with vegan Parmesan cheese.

Melanzana

I really enjoy eggplant, as it is very versatile. You can bread and fry it, slice into thick matchsticks, or cube it. Its texture can mimic meat in many recipes.

¾ cup cooked gluten-free bow tie or other shaped pasta
1 medium eggplant, peeled and cubed
4 tablespoons oil
4 cloves garlic, finely chopped
1 tablespoon vegan butter
3 cups fresh spinach, chopped
3 tablespoons fresh lemon juice
Salt and pepper to taste
¾ cup vegan Parmesan cheese, divided

Bring a large pot of lightly salted water to a boil. Add pasta and cook for 8 to 10 minutes or until al dente; drain. Keep warm.

Meanwhile, heat the oil and butter in a skillet over medium heat. Add the garlic; cook and stir until softened. Mix in the eggplant. Let the eggplant cook for 5 minutes without stirring too frequently, as too much stirring can break down the cubes. Cook until tender, about 5 more minutes.

Mix in the spinach and season with salt, and pepper. Cook, stirring occasionally, for 3 minutes. Stir in the drained pasta and lemon juice along with ½ cup of the Parmesan cheese. Transfer to a serving dish and top with remaining cheese.

Kale Puttanesca

Feel free to substitute any leafy green in place of kale. However, kale is a highly nutritious green, and very versatile, so I recommend eating kale as often as possible.

½ pound package gluten-free angel hair pasta
2 tablespoons oil
½ large onion, sliced
2 cloves garlic, minced
Pinch of red pepper flakes, optional
1 tablespoon drained capers
1 cup canned diced tomatoes, undrained
2 cups coarsely chopped kale or other greens
1 (4 ounce) can sliced black olives, drained
½ cup vegan Parmesan cheese

Bring a large pot of lightly salted water to a boil. Add pasta and cook for 8 to 10 minutes or until al dente; drain.

Meanwhile, heat oil in a large skillet over medium-high heat. Add onions, garlic, and red pepper flakes. Cook and stir until the onion has softened and begun to turn golden brown, about 5 minutes. Stir in capers and diced tomatoes, including juice, and bring to a simmer. Stir in kale, and simmer over medium-low heat until wilted and tender, about 10 minutes.

Once the pasta has cooked and been drained, stir into the Puttanesca along with the black olives. Toss and sprinkle with vegan Parmesan cheese before serving.

Asparagus Pasta

1 ½ pounds fresh asparagus, trimmed and cut into 1 inch pieces

¼ cup vegetable broth

½ pound fresh mushrooms, sliced

8 ounces gluten-free angel hair or other pasta

½ cup vegan Parmesan cheese

½ cup lemon juice

Bring a large pot of lightly salted water to a boil. Add angel hair pasta, cook for 5 to 6 minutes, until al dente; drain.

Heat the vegetable stock in a skillet over medium heat, and cook the garlic for 1 to 2 minutes. Add the asparagus, mushrooms, and tomatoes, stirring to coat, and continue cooking uncovered 10 minutes, or until the asparagus is tender, according to your personal taste preference.

Place the pasta in a large bowl, and toss with lemon juice. Add the asparagus and tomato mixture. Serve pasta with shredded cheese.

Lentils and Pasta

This recipe is very hearty and filling and gets more flavorful when leftover and reheated the next day.

1 onion, chopped
3 cloves garlic, minced
2 tablespoons oil
1 (19 ounce) can vegan lentil soup, such as Amy's
1 cup crushed tomatoes
1 (10 ounce) package frozen chopped spinach
1 (16 ounce) package small shaped gluten-free pasta
Salt and pepper to taste
2 tablespoons vegan Parmesan cheese
8ounces gluten-free pasta of choice

Cook pasta according to package instructions, drain.

Brown onion and garlic in oil over medium heat. Stir in lentil soup and tomatoes. Bring to boil. Stir in spinach and spices. Simmer 5 minutes. Mix pasta into lentil sauce. Serve with Parmesan cheese.

Pasta with Spinach

This dish appeals to many who do not normally care for spinach, so you may be able to get your children to eat this without a hassle. For me, you can never have too much spinach in this recipe, so you can double the amount if you are a spinach fan.

8 ounces gluten-free penne pasta
2 tablespoons oil
3 cups fresh chopped tomatoes
10 ounces (or more) fresh spinach, washed and chopped
1 clove garlic, minced
8 ounces shredded Mozzarella cheese
Salt and pepper to taste

Cook pasta according to package directions. Drain, and set aside.

Heat oil in a large pot. Add tomatoes, spinach, and garlic; cook and stir 2 minutes, or until spinach is wilted and mixture is thoroughly heated.

Add pasta and cheese; cook 1 minute. Season to taste with salt and pepper.

Pasta with Greens and Pine Nuts

Broccoli Raab was readily available on the East Coast, but much harder for me to find now that I live in the Midwest. If you too have trouble obtaining it, I suggest turnip greens as a substitute, along with some small cut broccoli florets.

½ bunch Rapini (Broccoli Raab)
½ bunch Swiss chard
¼ cup oil
3 cloves garlic, minced
1 leek, white part only, sliced thinly
1 cup vegetable stock
1 pinch salt and pepper, to taste
1 pound gluten-free pasta of choice
3 tablespoons toasted pine nuts

Trim the flower ends off the rapini, leaving 2 inches of stem. Set aside. Cut the remaining stems into 1 inch pieces. Set aside.
Cut the chard into 1 inch slices. Reserve the leafy part with the rapini flowers and the stems with the rapini stems.

In a large skillet, heat the oil over medium heat and add the garlic. When the garlic is browned, remove it and discard.

Add the leeks to the oil and cook until the leeks soften. Add the vegetable stems, the stock and the salt and pepper. Cover and cook 4 minutes. Add the chard leaves and rapini flowers and cook, covered, another 2 minutes.

Cook the pasta in boiling salted water until al dente.
Drain the pasta, return it to the pot and add the vegetable mixture.

Transfer to a serving dish and top with the pine nuts.

Pasta with Sun-Dried tomatoes

1 (16 ounce) package dry gluten-free pasta of choice
1 bunch Swiss chard, stems removed
2 tablespoons oil
½ cup dried ***or*** oil-packed sun-dried tomatoes, chopped
½ cup pitted, chopped Kalamata olives
½ cup pitted, chopped green olives
1 clove garlic, minced
¼ cup fresh vegan Parmesan cheese

Bring a large pot of lightly salted water to a boil. Stir in pasta, cook for 10 to 12 minutes, until al dente, and drain.

Place chard in a microwave safe bowl. Fill bowl about ½ full with water. Cook on High in the microwave 2 minutes, until wilted; drain.

Heat the oil in a skillet over medium heat. Stir in the sun-dried tomatoes, Kalamata olives, green olives, and garlic. Mix in the chard. Cook and stir until tender. Toss with pasta and sprinkle with vegan Parmesan cheese and serve.

Beany Pasta

8 ounces uncooked gluten-free spiral pasta
1 small onion, chopped
2 garlic cloves, minced
1 bunch escarole or spinach, trimmed and coarsely chopped
1 (15 ounce) can white kidney (Cannelini) beans, rinsed and drained
1 cup vegetable broth
1/3 cup grated vegan Parmesan cheese

Cook pasta according to package directions, drain.

Meanwhile, in a large skillet, cook onion and garlic until onion is tender; drain.

Stir in escarole, beans and broth. Cover and simmer for 6-8 minutes or until escarole is wilted and tender.

Drain pasta; add to vegetable mixture. Sprinkle with cheese.

Creamy Cheesy Angel Hair

This is a rich, creamy recipe, and is best served in a small portions offset with soup and salad.

8 ounces gluten-free angel hair pasta
1 (14.5 ounce) can diced tomatoes
2 cups baby spinach leaves
½ cup vegan sour cream
½ cup shredded vegan Mozzarella cheese
½ cup vegan Parmesan cheese
1 tablespoon prepared basil pesto (optional)

Bring a large pot of lightly salted water to a boil. Add the pasta and cook for 3 to 4 minutes, until tender. Drain.

While you wait for the pasta, combine the tomatoes and spinach in a saucepan over medium heat.

When the spinach begins to wilt, stir in the sour cream, cheeses, and optional pesto. Toss sauce with pasta and serve immediately.

Tempeh Carbonara

2 tablespoons of oil
4 shallots, diced
1 large onion, cut into thin strips
1 package of tempeh, cut into small strips
1 clove garlic, chopped
1 (16 ounce) package gluten-free fettuccini pasta
½ cup Mimic crème ***or*** vegan sour cream
¾ cup vegan Parmesan cheese
Salt and pepper to taste

Heat olive oil in a large heavy saucepan over medium heat. Sauté shallots until softened. Stir in onion and tempeh, and cook until tempeh is evenly browned. Stir in garlic and remove from heat.

Bring a large pot of lightly salted water to a boil. Add pasta and cook for 8 to 10 minutes or until al dente. Drain pasta, then return it to the pot.

In a medium bowl, whisk together cream, and vegan Parmesan. Pour the tempeh mixture over the pasta, then stir in the cream mixture. Season with salt and pepper.

Zucchini Pasta

1 pound gluten-free rotini pasta
5 small zucchini, sliced
1/3 cup olive oil
4 cloves garlic, minced
1 pinch crushed red pepper flakes
1/3 cup chopped fresh parsley
Salt and pepper to taste
½ cup vegan Parmesan cheese

Bring a large pot of lightly salted water to a boil. Add pasta and cook according to package instructions. Add zucchini to boiling water for the last 1-2 minutes (or until desired tenderness) to the water. You can also sauté, steam, or prepare the zucchini in any manner desired.

In a large skillet, sauté garlic in oil and hot pepper flakes. Add drained zucchini and parsley, then mix all together and simmer for 5 to 10 minutes.

Toss with pasta; then add cheese and salt and pepper to taste, and serve.

Buttery Herb Pasta

½ pound uncooked gluten-free pasta of choice
½ cup vegan buttery spread, such as Earth Balance
4 cloves garlic, minced
3 tablespoons chopped fresh basil
1 tablespoon dried oregano
1 tablespoon chopped fresh parsley
Salt and pepper to taste
2 tablespoons sliced black olives

Cook pasta according to the package directions. Drain the pasta and transfer to a large bowl.

Meanwhile, melt the butter or margarine over medium heat. Stir in the garlic and cook for a couple of minutes. Stir in the herbs. Add the butter mixture and toss. Season with salt and pepper. Sprinkle with black olive slices and serve.

Broccoli Pasta

8 ounces uncooked gluten-free spaghetti
2 cups fresh broccoli florets
2 large tomatoes, peeled, seeded, and diced
2 garlic cloves, minced
¼ teaspoon crushed red pepper flakes
2 tablespoons oil
½ cup sliced black olives
¼ cup vegan Parmesan cheese
Salt and pepper to taste

In a large skillet or Dutch oven, bring 3 quarts water to a boil. Add spaghetti; boil, and cook until almost done. Add broccoli to the boiling pasta for the last 2 minutes to cooking time, or steam separately until desired texture.

Meanwhile, in a nonstick skillet, sauté the tomatoes, garlic and pepper flakes in oil for 2 minutes. Drain pasta mixture; add to the skillet. Add remaining ingredients and toss to coat.

Eggplant and Spaghetti

2 tablespoons oil
1 eggplant, peeled and cut into ½ -inch cubes
1 (28 ounce) can crushed tomatoes
2 tablespoons minced fresh basil
1 ¼ teaspoons granulated sweetener
1 (7 ounce) jar roasted red peppers, drained and cut into strips
1 (16 ounce) package gluten-free spaghetti
2 tablespoons vegan butter
½ cup vegan Parmesan cheese
Salt and pepper to taste

Heat the oil in a skillet over medium heat, and cook the eggplant about 10 minutes. Stir in the tomatoes, basil, pepper, and sweetener. Simmer, stirring occasionally, 45 minutes.

Mix the roasted red peppers into the skillet with the eggplant mixture. Continue cooking until eggplant is the consistency of the rest of the sauce.

Bring a large pot of lightly salted water to a boil. Place pasta in the pot, and cool until al dente, and drain. Serve the eggplant and tomato sauce over the cooked spaghetti.

Homemade Manicotti

I had such a hard time finding already-made manicotti, that I finally had to work on a recipe from scratch.
This is the most complicated recipe in this cookbook, and practice makes perfect. I suggest practicing with making and especially folding the shells, and then when you have this mastered, you can proceed to make this for your favorite holiday meal.

Ingredients for Manicotti Noodles

1 cup gluten-free all-purpose flour
1 ¼ cups plain milk product
9 tablespoons mashed tofu
½ teaspoon xanthan or guar gum

Ingredients for Filling

1 package silken tofu (16oz)
1 tbsp Vegan Parmesan
1 teaspoon of dried basil
½ teaspoon garlic powder
1 egg replcacer portion, prepared according to package

Ingredients – Other
1 jar or portion of your favorite tomato sauce
non-stick spray or oil as needed

For the shells: Add the flour and xanthan gum to a large mixing bowl. Add the mashed tofu and water, then stir until blended. The batter should be rather thin, like pancakes.

Heat a small frying pan over medium heat and coat with non-stick spray or oil. Add a small amount of batter to the pan and quickly tilt the pan so the batter evenly covers the entire bottom of the pan in a thin layer, much like if you were making crepes or pancakes. Cook about 2 minutes until the top of the batter is dry, then turn over carefully and cook the other side. Set aside to cool. Place parchment or other paper in between each manicotti shell to prevent sticking. and repeat until you are out of batter.

For the filling: Combine all of the filling ingredients in a mixing bowl and stir until combined and resembling ricotta. Do not over mash.

To assemble: Coat bottom of the pan with just a little bit of tomato sauce diluted with water. Hold a cooled shell in the palm of one hand and add about 3 tablespoons of filling lengthwise across the center of the shell. Flip one side and then the other over the filling to fold. Flip the tube over (so the folds are on the bottom) and place carefully into the baking pan. Repeat with the remaining shells and filling.

Cover the manicotti with your favorite tomato sauce. Bake uncovered at 350°for 45 minutes.

Portabella Penne

1 (8 ounce) package uncooked gluten-free penne pasta
2 tablespoons oil
½ pound portabella mushrooms, thinly sliced
½ cup vegan margarine
½ cup gluten-free all-purpose flour
1 large clove garlic, minced
½ teaspoon dried basil
2 cups milk product
2 cups vegan Mozzarella cheese
1 (10 ounce) package frozen chopped spinach, thawed
¼ cup gluten-free soy sauce

Preheat oven to 350°F. Lightly grease a 9x13 inch baking dish.

Bring a large pot of water to a boil. Place pasta in the pot, cook until al dente, and drain.

Heat the oil in a saucepan over medium heat. Stir in the mushrooms, cook 1 minute, and set aside. Melt margarine in the saucepan.

Mix in flour, garlic, and basil. Gradually mix in milk until thickened. Stir in 1 cup cheese until melted.

Remove saucepan from heat, and mix in cooked pasta, mushrooms, spinach, and soy sauce. Transfer to the prepared baking dish, and top with remaining cheese.

Bake 20 minutes until bubbly and lightly brown.

Basic Tomato Sauce

This is a good all purpose sauce that works well with or without the onions and peppers. You can make it chunkier, sweeter, or spicier as desired. I make a large batch and then freeze for later.

1 (28 ounce) can stewed tomatoes
1 (28 ounce) can crushed tomatoes
2 yellow onions, chopped
2 green bell peppers, chopped
2 cloves garlic, chopped
2 tablespoons agave nectar or sweetener of choice
1 tablespoon dried basil
½ teaspoon dried oregano
Salt and pepper to taste

Blend the stewed tomatoes and crushed tomatoes in a blender. In a stock pot or large kettle, sauté onions, peppers, and garlic.

Pour in tomatoes, and reduce heat. Add agave/sweetener, basil and oregano, and simmer about 40 minutes.

Season with salt and pepper before serving.

Primavera

This is a different version of a recipe I published in the Virtuous Vegan. This one seems more "springtime" as the name implies, but of course, I love them both equally.

1 (12 ounce) package gluten-free penne pasta
1 yellow squash, chopped
1 zucchini, chopped
1 carrot, julienned
½ red bell pepper, julienned
½ pint cherry or grape tomatoes
1 cup fresh green beans, trimmed and cut into 1 inch pieces
5 spears asparagus, trimmed and cut into 1 inch pieces
¼ cup olive oil, divided
Salt and pepper, to taste
½ tablespoon lemon juice
1 tablespoon Italian seasoning
1 tablespoon vegan butter
¼ large yellow onion, thinly sliced
2 cloves garlic, minced
1/3 cup chopped fresh basil leaves
1/3 cup chopped fresh parsley
3 tablespoons balsamic vinegar
½ cup vegan Parmesan cheese

Preheat oven to 450°F. Line a baking sheet with aluminum foil.

Bring a large pot of water to a boil. Add penne pasta and cook until al dente; drain.

In a bowl, toss squash, zucchini, carrot, red bell pepper, tomatoes, green beans, and asparagus with 2 tablespoons olive oil, salt, pepper, lemon juice, and Italian seasoning. Arrange vegetables on the baking sheet, and roast 15 minutes, until tender.

Heat remaining olive oil and butter in a large skillet. Stir in the onion and garlic, and cook until tender. Mix in cooked pasta, basil, parsley, and balsamic vinegar.

Gently toss and cook until heated through. Remove from heat and transfer to a large bowl. Toss with roasted vegetables and sprinkle with cheese to serve.

Homemade Gluten-Free Pasta

Having trouble finding gluten-free pasta in your area? Why not just make your own? It is not quite as hard as the manicotti recipe, and for those who used to enjoy the art of homemade pasta making, this is a real treat. I suggest also experimenting with various gluten-free flours for different flavors and textures. I find this one to be the most all-purpose, but I also enjoy brown rice, quinoa, and amaranth pasta.

2/3 cup potato flour
2 tablespoons tapioca starch
½ teaspoon salt
1 tablespoon xanthan gum
2 portions of egg replacer, prepared according to instructions
1 tablespoon oil

Combine flour, starches, salt and gum. Prepare egg replacer and add oil. Pour this mixture into flour mixture and stir. Work together into a firm ball.

Knead for a minute or two. Place ball of dough on a board or lightly floured surface and roll as thin as possible. You will know you have the right thinness and texture if the dough is tough and although almost transparent, will still handle well.

Slice the noodles into very thin strips, or if using for lasagna, into 1-1/2" x 4" rectangles. The pasta is now ready to cook or to freeze uncooked for later use.

Cook the pasta in salted boiling water to which 1 tablespoon of oil has been added, for 10 to 20 minutes depending on the thickness and the size of your pieces.

Fettuccine Alfredo

A fairly rich and heavy dish, you may prefer this as a side dish than a main course. I like to add bulky vegetables such as mushrooms and artichokes, but you can use any vegetable(s) you like, or omit.

1 pound gluten-free fettuccine

1 cup vegan butter

2 cups of Mimic Crème or unflavored milk product

1 teaspoon of nutritional yeast

1 package of vegan cream cheese

2 cups vegan Parmesan cheese

½ cup vegan sour cream

2 cups vegan Mozzarella

Bring a large pot of water to a boil. Add fettuccine and cook according to package instructions. Drain and coat with a small amount of vegan butter or oil to help prevent sticking.

While pasta is cooking, prepare the sauce. In a large saucepan, melt butter into crème/milk product over low heat. Stir in cheeses over medium heat until melted. Stir in the sour cream and heat until warm. Add pasta to sauce. Serve immediately.

Specialty Lasagna

You can either make traditional layered lasagna, or roll-ups with this creamy, yet rich tomato pink sauce. Either way, this is one of my favorite meals by far, feeds a crowd, and freezes well.

1 (16 ounce) package gluten-free lasagna noodles

1 bag fresh spinach leaves, or other greens (optional)

1 cup sliced mushrooms, or other vegetable

2 cloves garlic, minced

2 tablespoons vegetable oil

1 jar pasta sauce of choice, or our Basic recipe

5 tablespoons vegan butter

2 (28 ounce) cans crushed tomatoes, drained

3 cups Mimic Crème or other milk product

1 cup vegan Parmesan

1 teaspoon dried basil

1 pound of firm tofu, drained and mashed

4 cups shredded vegan Mozzarella cheese

Cook the lasagna noodles in a large pot of boiling water for 10 minutes, or until al dente. Rinse with cold water, and drain.

To make the sauce, sauté garlic in the butter in a large skillet. Add cream/milk and cook for 3 minutes or until just until warm, stirring frequently to prevent burning. Pour in tomatoes, sauce, Parmesan, basil, and 1 cup Mozzarella cheese, cooking until cheese melts.

In a large saucepan, cook and stir mushrooms, spinach, or other vegetables in oil for about 3 minutes. Stir into the sauce, reduce heat, and simmer 15 minutes.

Prepare the filling by mixing together the tofu and 2 cups Mozzarella cheese. Set aside. Preheat oven to 350°F.

Spread 1 cup tomato sauce into the bottom of a greased 9x13 inch baking dish. Layer ½ each, lasagna noodles, tofu mix, sauce, and Mozzarella cheese. Repeat layering, and top with remaining cheese. Bake, uncovered, for 40 minutes. Let stand 15 minutes before serving.

Italian Risotto

Italian risotto is a recipe my mother had little patience to prepare, but often enjoy at a friend's. Whether served as an entree or side dish, I discovered it is easier to prepare than you might think.

For variety, you can always add in some extra vegetables, if you prefer, to reflect what is in season. This vegetarian risotto recipe is creamy and will be a crowd pleaser for your non-vegan friends.

3 tablespoons oil

8 cups vegetable broth (you may not need all of this)

2 cups arborio rice, dry

Salt and pepper to taste

1 cup vegan Parmesan cheese

In a large skillet, heat the oil and add the arborio rice, stirring constantly, for 3 to 4 minutes.

Add about a half cup of the vegetable broth to the rice, stirring frequently. When most of the liquid has absorbed, add another half cup of broth. Continue adding broth, a bit at a time, until the rice is done cooking, about 20 minutes. You may not need all of the broth, so do not add more than what is really needed.

Pasta with Cabbage

This simple dish is one of my favorites with a sprinkle of vegan cheese on top and breadsticks.

3 cups vegetable broth

1 pound gluten-free linguine

6 cups green cabbage, shredded

2 tablespoons oil

3 cloves garlic, minced

A pinch of red pepper flakes, optional

Salt and pepper to taste

Bring a pot of salted water to boil and cook the linguine according to package directions.

While pasta is cooking, heat olive oil in a large skillet over medium heat. Add garlic and sauté for three minutes, stirring constantly. Add cabbage and toss to combine.

Add remaining vegetable broth, cover, and steam over medium-low heat for 5 minutes, until the cabbage is tender but not mushy.

Drain pasta and add to skillet. Toss well and season to taste with salt and pepper.

Polenta Pizza Casserole

2 rolls of precooked polenta (in the produce section)
2 tablespoons of water
2 tablespoons of cornstarch
2 tablespoons gluten-free all-purpose flour
1 pinch of garlic powder
½ cup vegan Parmesan cheese
½ cup vegan Mozzarella cheese
2 cups of tomato sauce
½ medium green pepper, cut into strips
½ cup sliced mushrooms
½ cup sliced black olives

Preheat oven to 450F. Spray pizza pan with nonstick cooking spray.

Slice polenta, and place in food processor. Process polenta, and add water, cornstarch, flour, garlic and 1/2 cup vegan Parmesan cheese. Blend until smooth. Spread polenta evenly on pizza pan.

Bake for 15 minutes. Remove polenta from oven, and spread 2 cups sauce evenly over polenta crust. Top with sliced mushrooms, bell peppers, scallions and vegan Mozzarella cheese.

Return to oven and bake 25 minutes. Remove from oven, and let stand for 5 minutes before serving.

Vegetables

Zucchini Stir Fry

1 tablespoon of oil

4 cups sliced zucchini

1 onion, chopped

1 teaspoon of dried basil leaves

3 tomatoes, sliced

Salt and pepper to taste

1 cup shredded vegan cheddar cheese

Heat oil in heavy skillet or wok. Add zucchini and onion; stir fry 3-4 minutes until onion is crisp tender. Add seasonings.

Layer tomatoes over vegetables and sprinkle cheese over all. Cook over medium heat 2-3 minutes until cheese is melted. Serve over hot cooked rice. 4 servings

Zucchini Bake

5 cups sliced zucchini (usually 2 large)
2 portions of egg replacer, made with ½ cup milk product
1 cup gluten-free all-purpose flour (seasoned to taste)
3 cups pasta sauce of choice
2 packages (16oz total) of vegan Mozzarella cheese
5 medium sized ripe tomatoes, sliced
½ cup vegan Parmesan cheese

Preheat oven to 350°F.

Peel and slice, if desired, enough zucchini to measure out to 5 cups. Season flour mix with oregano, basil, and/or other spices as desired. Mix 1/2 cup of milk product with egg replacer. Dip zucchini slices into egg bath and then into flour.

Spray cookie sheet with cooking spray. Place battered zucchini on cookie sheet and bake until soft or desired tenderness, approximately 10 minutes. Remove from oven.

Cover the bottom of a 9x13 baking dish with pasta sauce and a layer of zucchini slices. Top with sauce and tomato slices and cheese. Repeat. Top with remaining sauce and Parmesan cheese and bake at for an additional 30 minutes, or until sauce and cheese are bubbly.

Marinated Mushrooms and Peppers

½ cup red wine vinegar

1/3 cup water

2 tablespoons oil

1 teaspoon granulated sweetener

1 tablespoon chopped onion

1 tablespoon chopped fresh parsley

½ teaspoon dried basil

2 cloves garlic, minced

Salt and pepper to taste

2 pounds of fresh mushrooms, stems removed

½ red bell pepper, diced

Combine the vinegar, water, oil, sweetener, onion, parsley, basil, garlic, salt, and pepper in a saucepan. Bring to a boil and stir in the mushrooms and red pepper. Return mixture to a boil; reduce heat and simmer until the mushrooms are tender, 5 to 10 minutes.

Remove from heat and allow to cool to room temperature. Transfer to a covered container and store in refrigerator at least 4 hours before serving.

Escarole and Olives

This simple yet elegant dish can be served as either a main course or side dish.

3 tablespoons of oil

2 medium heads escarole or other greens – rinsed and chopped

½ cup lemon juice

1 pinch salt and pepper

10 Kalamata olives, pitted and sliced

Heat oil in a wok over high heat. Add escarole/greens; cook and stir until greens begin to wilt. Stir in lemon juice. Add salt, pepper, and olives; cook and stir for another minute. Serve immediately.

Stewed Tomatoes

This is a great recipe to make in the peak of summer. For those of you are canning enthusiasts, feel free to jar your own to have for the rest of the year.

24 large tomatoes - peeled, seeded and chopped

1 cup chopped celery

½ cup chopped onion

¼ cup chopped green bell pepper

2 teaspoons dried basil

1 tablespoon granulated sweetener

In a large saucepan over medium heat, combine tomatoes, celery, onion, bell pepper, basil and sweetener.

Cover and cook for 10 minutes, stirring occasionally to prevent sticking.

Eggplant Parmesan

My favorite Italian food. You can omit the breading if you want to, but I really prefer it with the crumbs.

3 eggplants, peeled and thinly sliced

2 egg replacer portions, prepared according to package

½ cup milk product

4 cups Italian seasoned gluten-free bread crumbs

6 cups tomato sauce, divided

16 ounces vegan Mozzarella cheese, shredded and divided

½ cup vegan Parmesan cheese, divided

½ teaspoon dried basil

Preheat oven to 350°F. Prepare egg replacer and add milk. Dip eggplant slices in egg replacer mixture, then in bread crumbs. Place in a single layer on a baking sheet. Bake for 5 minutes on each side.

In a 9x13 inch baking dish, spread sauce to cover the bottom. Place a layer of eggplant slices on top. Sprinkle with Mozzarella and Parmesan cheeses. Repeat with remaining ingredients, ending with the cheeses. Sprinkle basil on top. Bake for 35 minutes, or until golden brown.

Italian Greens

1 bunch kale/greens, stems removed, leaves coarsely chopped

1 clove garlic, minced

1 tablespoon of oil

2 tablespoons of balsamic vinegar

Salt and pepper to taste

Cook the kale in a large, covered saucepan over medium-high heat until the leaves wilt. Once the kale wilts, uncover and stir in the garlic, olive oil and vinegar. Cook while stirring for 2 more minutes. Add salt and pepper to taste.

Broccoli Cheese Bake

1 ½ pounds fresh broccoli spears, cut into ¼ inch slices

1 cup mashed tofu

2 egg replacer portions, prepared according to instructions

½ cup vegan Parmesan cheese

3 tablespoons gluten-free all-purpose flour

½ teaspoon Italian seasoning

¾ cup tomato sauce

1 cup shredded vegan Mozzarella cheese

In a large saucepan, bring 8 cups water to a boil. Add broccoli and salt; cover and boil for 5 minutes. Drain and pat dry.

Preheat oven to 375°F.

In a blender, combine the tofu, prepared egg replacer, Parmesan cheese, flour and Italian seasoning; cover and process until smooth.

Place half of the broccoli in a casserole or baking dish coated with nonstick cooking spray; top with half of the tofu mixture. Repeat layers. Spoon sauce over the top; sprinkle with Mozzarella cheese. Bake, uncovered for 25-30 minutes or until bubbly.

Italian Potato Cakes

1 medium potato, peeled and grated

2 tablespoons chopped onion

2 tablespoons gluten-free all-purpose flour

1 egg replacer portion, prepared according to instructions

¼ teaspoon dried basil

¼ teaspoon dried oregano

Salt and pepper to taste

1 tablespoon of oil

Shredded vegan Mozzarella cheese

Rinse grated potato in cold water; drain thoroughly. In a bowl, combine potato, onion, flour, egg replacer, basil, oregano, salt and pepper. In a skillet, heat oil; add potato mixture. Cover and cook over medium-low heat for 5-7 minutes or until golden brown. Turn; sprinkle with cheese. Cover and cook over low heat 5 minutes longer.

Roasted Cauliflower

1 head cauliflower, cut into florets

1 large red bell pepper, cut into 1-1/2 inch pieces

1 red onion, sliced

3 tablespoons balsamic vinegar

2 tablespoons red wine vinegar

2 teaspoons of oil

Salt and pepper to taste

Combine the cauliflower, bell pepper, onion, balsamic vinegar, wine vinegar, and oil in a large bowl and stir well. Allow to marinate in refrigerator 1 to 2 hours.

Preheat oven to 450°F.

Season vegetables with salt and pepper. Pour into a 9x13 baking dish. Bake until tender, about 30 minutes, stirring occasionally.

Milano Brussel Sprouts

3 cups tomato juice

1 pound Brussels sprouts, trimmed

2 tablespoons of oil

2 cloves garlic, minced

1 teaspoon oregano

Salt and pepper to taste

1 large tomato, diced

½ cup vegan Parmesan

Bring the tomato juice to a boil in a large saucepan. Add Brussels sprouts and cook for 5 to 7 minutes. They should still be slightly firm. Drain, and rinse with cold water.

Slice the sprouts in half, and set aside. Heat one tablespoon of oil in a large skillet over medium-high heat. Add the garlic and tomatoes; cook and stir for about 5 minutes. Add the remaining oil and Brussels sprouts. Reduce the heat to medium and cook, stirring until the sprouts are well coated with the flavor. Season with salt and pepper, and cook for 5 more minutes before serving. Top with cheese.

Italian Succotash

2 tablespoons of oil

1 tablespoon of vegan margarine

1 small onion, chopped

¼ cup milk product

1 cup of vegetable stock

8 ounces firm tofu, drained and cubed

1 (6.5 ounce) jar marinated artichokes, drained

2 cloves garlic, minced

2 (15 ounce) cans of corn, drained

In a large saucepan over medium heat, heat oil and margarine. Stir in ½ the onion, and sauté until tender. Add ½ cup of stock and stir in corn, and heat another 5 minutes.

In a medium saucepan over medium heat, lightly brown the tofu and remaining onion in the remaining stock. Stir in the garlic.

Remove from heat, and mix in the tofu, artichoke hearts, and corn. Can be served hot or cold.

Baked Fennel

Fennel is a unique vegetable that has a wonderful flavor in this casserole. If you are not familiar with fennel, it is wonderful for digestion, and therefore I suggest using it as a tea, appetizer, or light meal regularly.

2 fennel bulbs

1 tablespoon of vegan butter

¾ cup Mimic Crème or plain milk product

¾ cup vegan sour cream

¼ cup vegan Parmesan cheese

Preheat the oven to 400°F. Cut the base off of the fennel bulbs, and cut a cone shape into the base to remove the core. You can see the core because it is whiter than the surrounding green. This is optional, but helps the fennel cook faster. Slice the fennel vertically (upright) into ¼ inch thick slices.

Melt the butter in a large skillet over medium heat. Add the fennel, and fry for about 5 minutes. Stir in the crème/milk and sour cream until well blended. Transfer to a shallow baking dish. Sprinkle Parmesan cheese over the top.

Bake for 30 minutes in the preheated oven, or until the top is golden brown and the fennel is tender enough to pierce with a fork.

Asparagus Romano

1 bunch asparagus spears, ends trimmed

2 tablespoons of vegan butter

1 (8 ounce) package sliced mushrooms

1 onion, minced

½ teaspoon garlic powder

½ teaspoon dried basil

Salt and pepper to taste

½ cup vegan Parmesan cheese

Steam the asparagus spears in a basket-style steamer over boiling water until tender, 5 to 10 minutes. Drain and remove to a serving dish; keep warm.

Meanwhile, melt half of the butter in a large skillet over medium-high heat. Stir in the sliced mushrooms, and cook until they brown. Transfer to a serving dish, and set aside. Melt the remaining butter in the skillet, and stir in the onions. Cook until the onions soften and turn translucent, about 3 minutes. Season with garlic powder, basil, salt and pepper.

Sprinkle the onion mixture with half of the Parmesan cheese, and stir in the reserved mushrooms. Pour over the asparagus in the serving dish and sprinkle with remaining cheese.

Veggie Stuffed Peppers

This is a grain-free and fresh twist on stuffed peppers. As such, feel free to serve with risotto, pasta, or your favorite bread.

1 green bell pepper, halved and seeded

1 red bell pepper, halved and seeded

1 yellow bell pepper, halved and seeded

1 pint cherry tomatoes, halved

½ cup chopped fresh basil leaves

2 cloves garlic, thinly sliced

Salt and pepper to taste

Preheat the oven to 400°F. Grease a 9x13 inch baking dish with cooking spray or oil of choice.

Place the bell pepper halves open side up in the prepared baking dish. In a medium bowl, toss together the cherry tomatoes, basil, and garlic. Fill each pepper half with a handful of this mixture. Season with salt and pepper. Cover the dish with aluminum foil.

Bake for 15 minutes , then remove the aluminum foil, and continue baking for an additional 15 minutes. These are equally good served hot or cold.

Cookies and Desserts

Florentines

2 cups of almonds, chopped fine

1 tablespoon rice flour

1 tablespoon cornstarch

2 teaspoons grated orange zest

¾ cup granulated sugar product

½ cup vegan butter, cut into pieces

1/3 cup Mimic cream or vegan condensed milk

2 tablespoons agave nectar

8 ounces vegan chocolate chips

Preheat the oven to 350˚F, positioning the rack in the center of the oven.

Line a heavy large baking sheet with parchment paper.

In a medium bowl, mix almonds, flour, and zest.

Heat a saucepan to medium heat and stir the sugar, butter, cream, and honey until the sugar dissolves. Bring the mixture to a boil and then remove from heat.

Stir in the almond mixture. Cool for 20 minutes, stirring occasionally. Using 2 teaspoons of batter for each, spoon 8 mounds of the batter onto the prepared baking sheet and flatten each one slightly with your finger.

Bake the cookies about 10 minutes until they are lacy (holes in them) and golden brown.

Slide parchment paper with cookies to a rack to cool completely. Then transfer the cookies to paper towels. Repeat with the remaining batter.

FREEZING: Cool completely and put in an airtight container in your freezer for up to two months. Defrost before continuing with recipe.

SANDWICH COOKIES: Stir the chocolate in a double boiler (or bowl set over simmering water) until the chocolate melts. Spread the melted chocolate over the bottom of 1 cookie and then sandwich with another cookie. Repeat with the remaining cookies.

Tri-Color Wedding Cookies

I used to love these as a kid, but didn't love how they made me feel afterwards. Of course, now I know what food sensitivities are, so this recipe is a far better choice for me.

8 ounces almond paste

1½ cups vegan butter, softened

1 cup granulated sweetener

½ cup mashed tofu

2 egg replacer portions, prepared according to instructions

1 teaspoon almond extract

2 cups gluten-free all-purpose flour

¼ teaspoon salt

5 drops green food coloring

5 drops yellow food coloring

5 drops red food coloring

1 (12 ounce) jar seedless raspberry jam, heated

1 (12 ounce) package vegan chocolate chips, melted

Preheat oven to 350°F.

Break almond paste into a large bowl, and beat in butter, sweetener, egg replacer, mashed tofu, and almond extract until light and fluffy. Beat in the flour and salt.

Split batter into three equal portions, mixing one portion with green food coloring, one with yellow, and one with red.

Spread each portion out to ¼ inch thickness into the bottom of an ungreased 9x13 inch baking pan.

Bake each layer for 12 to 15 minutes in the preheated oven, until lightly browned. Allow to cool.

On a cookie sheet or cutting board, stack the cakes, spreading tops of the first two layers with raspberry jam. Spread melted chocolate over top of the third layer.

Chill in the refrigerator for 1 hour, or until jam and chocolate are firm. Slice into small rectangles to serve.

Fig Cookies

2 ½ cups gluten-free all-purpose flour

2 teaspoons xanthan or guar gum

1/3 cup granulated sweetener

¼ teaspoon baking powder

½ cup vegan shortening

2 tablespoons butter

½ cup milk product

1 portion of egg replacer, prepared according to instructions

1 ½ cups dried figs

¾ cup golden raisins

¼ cup slivered almonds

¼ cup granulated sweetener

¼ cup hot water

¼ teaspoon ground cinnamon

In a large mixing bowl, combine flour, 1/3 cup sweetener and baking powder. Cut in shortening and butter until mixture resembles small peas. Stir in the milk and egg replacer until the dough comes together. Divide dough into two pieces, wrap and refrigerate for about 2 hours or until easy to handle.

In a food processor or blender, grind the figs, raisins and almonds until they are coarsely chopped. In a medium bowl, stir together the ¼ cup of sweetener, hot water, and cinnamon. Stir in the fruit mixture, cover and set aside until the dough is ready.

Preheat oven to 350°F.

On a lightly floured surface, roll each piece of the dough out to a 12 inch square. Cut each piece into twelve 3x4 inch rectangles.

Using a heaping tablespoon of filling for each rectangle, spread filling along one of the short sides of the rectangle. Roll up from that side. Place rolls, seam side down, on an ungreased cookie sheet. Curve each roll slightly. Snip outer edge of the curve three times.

Bake for 20 to 25 minutes until golden brown.

Spicy Chocolate Chip "Meatball" Cookies

Horrible name, delicious cookie! This recipe makes a lot, and they freeze well for up to 3 months.

1 cup vegan butter or coconut oil

2 cups milk product

2 cups rice flour

2 cups garbanzo flour

2 cups cornstarch or other starch

¾ cup granulated sweetener

1 tablespoon xanthan or guar gum

½ cup unsweetened cocoa powder

1 ¼ teaspoons baking soda

½ teaspoon ground cinnamon

½ teaspoon ground nutmeg

½ teaspoon ground cloves

1 ¾ cups vegan chocolate chips

1 cup of chopped walnuts

Preheat oven to 350°F. Grease cookie sheets.

In a medium saucepan over medium heat, combine the butter and milk. Cook until melted, stirring occasionally. Set aside to cool.

In a large bowl, stir together the flour, sweetener, cocoa, baking soda, cinnamon, nutmeg, and cloves. Stir in the milk mixture by hand until the dough is firm and not sticky. Mix in the chocolate chips and walnuts. Roll the dough into 1 ½ inch balls and place onto the prepared cookie sheets.

Bake for 20 to 25 minutes, until firm. Remove from baking sheets to cool on wire racks. Glaze with an optional thin confectioners' icing when cool.

Chocolate Almond Biscotti

Biscotti simply means cookie in Italian, but in this case, I am referring to what Americans call Biscotti- the long, crunchy double based cookie.

½ cup coconut oil at room temperature

2/3 cup granulated sweetener

¼ cup unsweetened cocoa powder

2 teaspoons baking powder

1 teaspoon baking soda

1 teaspoon gum

2 egg replacer portions, prepared according to instructions

1 cup sorghum flour

¾ cup teff flour

4 ounces of vegan chocolate, chopped

¾ cup vegan chocolate chips

1 teaspoon almond extract

2 teaspoons guar or xanthan gum

In a large mixing bowl, cream butter and sweetener with an electric mixer until light and fluffy. Gradually beat in cocoa and baking powder. Beat for 2 minutes. Beat in the egg replacer. Stir in flour by hand. Mix in white chocolate and chocolate chips. Cover dough, and chill for about 10 minutes.

Preheat oven to 375°F. Divide dough into two parts, and roll each part into a 9 inch long log. Place logs on lightly greased cookie sheet, about 4 inches apart. Flatten slightly.

Bake for 20 to 25 minutes, or until toothpick inserted in center comes out clean. Cool on cookie sheet for 5 minutes, then carefully transfer to a wire rack to cool for one hour.

Cut each loaf into ½ inch wide diagonal slices. Place slices on an ungreased cookie sheet, and bake at 325°F for 9 minutes. Turn cookies over, and bake for 7 to 9 minutes. Cool completely, then store in an airtight container

Cannoli

Traditionally made with heavy dairy products and the shells in a pizzelle iron. Here, both are eliminated, but you will need a cannoli mold, available at most kitchen store and online.

2 egg replacer portions, prepared according to instructions

½ cup granulated sweetener

¼ cup melted vegan butter

¼ cup coconut oil

1 ½ cups gluten-free all-purpose flour

¼ teaspoon baking soda

1 teaspoon xanthan or guar gum

1 teaspoon ground cinnamon

1 tablespoon distilled white vinegar

3 tablespoons cold water

Filling

3 cups granulated sugar product
½ cup coconut oil or margarine at room temperature
¼ cup vanilla milk product
2 teaspoons of vanilla extract Filling
¼ cup vegan chocolate chips
1 teaspoon vanilla extract
½ cup pistachios

In a medium bowl, stir together the egg replacer, sweetener, melted butter and oil. Stir in the flour, baking soda and cinnamon. Then add the cold water and vinegar. Mix well until smooth.

On a lightly floured surface, roll out the dough to 1/8-inch thickness. With a cutter, cut out rounds 5-inches in diameter. In batches, as necessary, wrap each round onto a cannoli mold, sealing the edges with water.

In a deep sauté pan, heat the oil to 350° F. Fry the cannolis in batches until just golden brown and crisp, about 2 minutes. Drain on paper towels, let cool, then gently slip the molds from the cannolis.

In a medium bowl, mix together the filling ingredients, except for the chocolate chips and pistachios.

Mix margarine/coconut oil, milk, and vanilla. Blend in sweetener. Fold in the chocolate chips and pistachios. Use a pastry bag to pipe the filling into the shells.

Zeppole

The Italian version of funnel cakes!

2 quarts oil for frying

1 cup gluten-free all-purpose flour

2 teaspoons baking powder

1 pinch salt

1 ½ teaspoons granulated sweetener

2 replacer portions, prepared according to instructions

1 cup mashed tofu

¼ teaspoon vanilla extract

½ cup confectioners' sugar for dusting

Heat oil in a deep-fryer or large skillet to 375°F.

In a medium saucepan, combine the flour, baking powder, salt and sugar. Stir in the egg replacer, mashed tofu, and vanilla. Mix gently over low heat until combined. Batter will be sticky.

Drop by tablespoons into the hot oil a few at a time. Zeppole will turn over by themselves. Fry until golden brown, about 3 or 4 minutes. Drain in a paper sack and dust with confectioners' sugar. Serve warm.

Tiramsu

CAKE

1 (18.25 ounce) package gluten-free cake mix or your own recipe

1 teaspoon instant coffee powder

¼ cup coffee

FILLING

1 (8 ounce) container vegan cream cheese

½ cup confectioners' sugar

2 tablespoons strong coffee or espresso

FROSTING

2 cups mimic crème or other heavy vegan liquid coffee creamer

¼ cup confectioners' sugar

2 tablespoons strong coffee or espresso

1 tub vegan whipped cream topping (such as Tru-Whip)

GARNISH

2 tablespoons unsweetened cocoa powder

1 (1 ounce) square vegan chocolate

Preheat oven to 350°F. Grease and flour 3 (9 inch) pans.

Prepare the cake mix, or your own, according to package directions. Divide two thirds of batter between 2 pans. Stir instant coffee into remaining batter; pour into remaining pan.

Bake according to their instructions until a toothpick inserted comes out clean. Let cool in pan for 10 minutes, then turn out onto a wire rack and cool completely.

In a measuring cup, combine brewed coffee and 1 tablespoon coffee liqueur; set aside.

To make the filling: In a small bowl, using an electric mixer set on low speed, combine tofu, ½ cup confectioners' sugar and 2 tablespoons coffee liqueur or strong coffee; beat just until smooth. Cover with plastic wrap and refrigerate.

To make the frosting: In a medium bowl, using an electric mixer set on medium-high speed, beat the crème , ¼ cup confectioners' sugar and 2 tablespoons coffee liqueur/coffee until stiff. Fold ½ cup of cream mixture into filling mixture. Gently fold in Tru-Whip or other non-dairy whipped cream.

To assemble the cake: Place one plain cake layer on a serving plate. Using a thin skewer, poke holes in cake, about 1 inch apart. Pour one third of reserved coffee mixture over cake, then spread with half of the filling mixture. Top with coffee-flavored cake layer; poke holes in cake. Pour another third of the coffee mixture over the second layer and spread with the remaining filling. Top with remaining cake layer; poke holes in cake. Pour remaining coffee mixture on top. Spread sides and top of cake with frosting. Place cocoa in a sieve and lightly dust top of cake. Garnish with chocolate curls. Refrigerate at least 30 minutes before serving. To make the chocolate curls, use a vegetable peeler and run it down the edge of the chocolate bar.

Vegan Struffoli (Italian Vegan "Honey" Balls)

½ cup unsweetened milk product
¼ cup unsweetened applesauce
3 tablespoons vegan margarine, melted
2 teaspoons vanilla
2 teaspoon freshly squeezed orange juice (optional)
1 teaspoon freshly grated orange peel
1 teaspoon freshly grated lemon peel (optional)
2 ½ cups gluten-free all-purpose flour
½ cup granulated sweetener
3 teaspoon baking powder
½ teaspoon salt
2 cups vegetable oil for frying
1 to 2 cups agave nectar
gluten-free sprinkles, optional

In large bowl mix milk, applesauce, margarine, vanilla, fresh orange juice (optional), and grated orange peel and freshly grated lemon peel, if using.

In separate mixing bowl sift flour, granulated sweetener, baking powder, and salt until well combined. Pour dry ingredients into wet ingredients and mix gently until well combined. Dough will become crumbly so you've got to get your hands involved and gently knead dough until all flour is combined with batter. Dough will be moderately sticky.

In a medium frying pan, pour 1/2" of oil into the pan. Ideally you want enough oil to allow the balls to float and not burn on the bottom of the pan. Turn heat to medium.

Take dough and roll it into a thick log on a clean surface. Rip off strips of dough and roll into little logs about 1" thick. Make sure the dough is rolled hard so there are no creases and deformities (this will make sure the dough rises properly in the pan). Cut the log into 1/2" pieces (bite size) and put on a plate.

Drop pieces about 10 at a time into hot oil in frying pan. Cooking time takes less than a minute so pay attention. When the bottom has reached a light golden brown, flip the ball over with tongs to brown the other side. When both sides are lightly golden brown stack onto a serving plate. If balls begin burning, turn heat down a bit. Repeat this until all balls are finished.

When all balls are cooked and stacked (this is traditionally served at Christmas so it should resemble the cone shape of a Christmas tree) pour 1 to 2 cups agave nectar over the balls. This is a very sweet dish, so add agave nectar to taste. Add sprinkles if desired, and serve hot.

About the Author

Dawn Grey, PhD, is a Certified Holistic Health Practitioner and owner of the Aruna Center of Lawrence, Kansas. After discovering her lifelong health issues were the results of dairy, egg, and wheat sensitivities in 2001, she changed her diet and the scope of her consultation business to help others identify and manage their own sensitivities. Now, nine years later, she is healthier, leaner, and happier than ever before.

Dawn is available for personal wellness coaching by special appointment. For more information about being a distance client of the Aruna Center, please contact Dawn at **reikirays@yahoo.com**

For additional holistic and metaphysical services, please visit her website at **www.arunacenter.com**

In addition to this cookbook, Dawn is the author of ***New Dawn Kitchen: Gluten-Free, Vegan, and Easily Sugar-Free Desserts*** and ***The Virtuous Vegan.*** She is also the author of ***Insight Tarot*** and ***The Complete Usui Reiki Guide***.

For those interested in learning more about holistic and natural methods of health and healing, Dawn and her staff over accredited distance education courses at **www.reikiraysinstitute.com.**

Visit **www.newdawnkitchen.com** for some pictures of featured recipes in this book, as well as her Facebook page, the Virtuous Vegan.

Made in the USA
Lexington, KY
04 February 2011